The Artificial
Key to Success

Debunking all the Myths of Success

Robin K Mathew

Writer's Pocket

First published by Writer's Pocket in 2024

email: publish@writerspocket.com

ISBN-13: 978-93-6083-876-8

www.writerspocket.com

DEDICATION

"The Artificial Key to Success" is a scathing critique of a world that favors connections over talent, social media presence over substance, and bias over meritocracy. Dedicated to the unsung heroes of society, this book stands as a tribute to all those who have been overlooked, undervalued, and marginalized by society.

To the underdogs of society who never got a chance to shine in the mainstream areas of arts, literature, science, or any other field because they didn't have a godfather or a guiding hand to help them navigate the treacherous waters of the establishment.

To all those unrecognized talents and greatness who the world never realized because they didn't have the societal favoring conducive factors to bring them to the front stage.

To all those great writers who never got a chance to see their work published in the mainstream publishing houses because of the biases and predilections of the gatekeepers called literary agents and editors.

And now, in the modern world, to all those precious talents who are pushed to obscurity because they don't have the "x factor" of social media followers to push them or praise them through their social media handles.

Let this be a tribute to the forgotten people in this post-truth era, where stories and presented as history, and those who know nothing about life teach you how to live, while those who stand for humanity, truth, and science are pushed to the dark holes of obscurity.

This book is dedicated to all those who have been overlooked, undervalued, and marginalized by society. May their stories be heard, and their talents be recognized. In an era where truth is distorted and narratives are manipulated, where hate mongers garner more attention than champions of humanity and science, "The Artificial Key to Success" demands a reckoning with the injustices that have silenced the voices of the marginalized and overlooked. It is a call to arms for those who dare to challenge the status quo and strive for a world where talent, integrity, and truth reign supreme.

Yes, above all, this book is a humble book that tries to debunk the global self-improvement market, estimated to be worth $38.3 billion in 2022 and $41.2 billion in 2023. Yes, this book was constantly rejected by more than 100 editors and publishing houses worldwide. No one ever showed the courage to read the full manuscript. For them, my name and the title of the book itself was the parameter for rejection. Thanks to all those editors who ghosted me, including the CEOs of the top publishing houses who never replied to my emails and messages. Thanks to all those brave editors who could not properly say that they cannot publish my book and instead blocked me on WhatsApp. I still get bewildered when you call a book a literary work contributing to society and deny the fact that it is just a business. I will not be shocked to hear if a great movie celebrity with millions of followers writes a book on neurosurgery and the great publishing houses wait at her doorstep to get the manuscript actually written by a ghost writer.

Anyway, I have no hard feelings towards the countless editors who ghosted me. I still thank all those who didn't have the courage to say that my work was rejected and instead blocked me on WhatsApp and never replied to my emails or LinkedIn chats. I'm grateful to those who didn't have the straightforwardness to tell me a believable reason for their rejection. Thanks to all those who tried to rip off money from me. Yes, without you, I could not have polished this work like this. All those unfair acts from you really strengthened me.

Robin K Mathew

CONTENTS

Part I. Deconstructing Success: A Logical Inquiry Into The Motivation Myths

Part II. Rational Reverie: Unravelling History, People And Events Through Logical Dissection

Part III. Who Decides Your Fate?

Part IV. The Para Spaces

Part V. Unconventional Paths To Success

Part I.

Deconstructing Success: A Logical Inquiry Into The Motivation Myths

1. Great Stage Shows Of Motivation

The curtains open, and the audience eagerly awaits the start of the show. The grand auditorium is filled with anticipation as hundreds of people have gathered to hear the distinguished speaker share the secrets of success. Dressed in European style, the speaker exudes an air of celebrity as he steps onto the stage. With a confident and authoritative voice, he begins to speak.

"Do you want to succeed in life? Don't you long for wealth, like I have achieved? Wouldn't you desire a high standard of living, similar to mine?"

The audience is captivated by the speaker's words, hanging on to every sentence. He shares stories of successful individuals like Bill Gates, Barack Obama, Elon Musk, and Lionel Messi, revealing their secrets to success. He tells the audience that they too can achieve anything they set their minds to, as long as they are willing to work hard and never give up on their dreams.

On another stage, another opens his treasure trove of knowledge and revelations, discussing "Thirty Short Ways to Become a Millionaire." He offers advice on entrepreneurship, making money in the stock market, and highlights the crucial habits and mistakes of influential individuals. He even reveals the secret formula behind Ratan Tata's success, the most respected businessman in India.

From there, we go to the online training spree of another motivational speaker. Here she shares insights on being a good husband, lover, and student. Yes, she delivers the same online program at a mere cost of Rs 99.

Not just the three motivational speakers cover a wide range of topics, from business shortcuts and success strategies to personal development programs. The self-improvement industry is a huge business, valued at around 10 billion dollars in the United States alone.

Hey, wait a minute; there's a small problem unaddressed here. Amidst all the self-promotion and enticing advertisements, we never use the spirit of inquiry or questioning here. Obviously, these gurus conveniently omit some crucial details. For instance, have we asked them the question: what kind of business are they actually involved in? How did they amass such wealth? Do renowned figures in society know about these self-proclaimed experts? Are they successful persons in real life or are they just bluffing? Could it be that the luxurious lifestyles they showcase are merely rented for the purpose of their profile shooting? Moreover, if these millionaires are truly so accomplished and busy, why are they struggling to make money by selling these so-called secrets?

So now ask yourself the question. Can anyone mention the name of even a single millionaire who has attended motivational classes and drawn inspiration from them? Why do renowned figures like Tata, Birla, Bajaj, Godrej, or Ambani never disclose such secrets? What kind of work experience do these gurus possess? Have they founded any notable companies? What is their educational background? Yes, that is the main reason behind their success. No one is posing these fundamental questions to them.

Recently, I've noticed a surge of individuals claiming to teach others how to write books and become best-selling authors. One such individual claimed to guide others in writing a book and achieving a millionaire status. However, upon closer inspection, it was revealed that she had only authored two self-published books, with a modest Amazon best-selling ranking of 7800.

The rise of new generation gurus has led to a multitude of questions and concerns. While they may offer valuable advice and insights, it's essential to question their credibility and motives. It's crucial to look beyond the glamour and glitz they project and seek genuine guidance from credible sources if you need help in any area.

2. The Unscientific Motivation Industry

The Beginning

When did the motivational industry originate? Is this a recent phenomenon? No, like any other cult, it traces its roots back to the emergence of languages and civilization. As per the available evidence, the oldest known self-help book is "The Maxims of Ptahhotep," authored in ancient Egypt around 2400 BC. This book comprises teachings on leading a virtuous life, covering subjects like ethics, self-discipline, personality development, and more. While a self-help program offers insights into achieving a fulfilling life, let's delve into how this evolved into a billion-dollar industry.

"Think and Grow Rich," penned by Napoleon Hill in 1937, could be considered a forerunner among self-help books and motivational programs. Although the book predominantly underscores the importance of attaining financial success, it was marketed as a resource for personal growth and self-improvement, as Hill believed his philosophy could be universally applied. It gained recognition for being a guide that facilitates self-enhancement in various aspects of life.

According to Forbes magazine, this book has sold over 70 million copies, making it one of the best-selling books. This attests to its widespread influence, resonating with individuals seeking personal development and empowerment.

Now, let's scrutinize the claims made by Napoleon Hill. He and his cult followers claim that he drew inspiration from

Andrew Carnegie, the renowned billionaire businessman. Hill asserts in his writings that he had conducted interviews with numerous billionaires over 25 years to learn their secrets of success. However, these claims have been largely debunked. Andrew Carnegie himself has revealed that he never allowed Hill to meet him, and the so-called insights Hill claimed to possess were later exposed as baseless and untrue. "A lie will go round the world while truth is pulling its boots on," so the majority believed Hill's claim than the debunked information.

Before publishing this book, Hill led a rather humble life. Numerous historians and law authorities have confirmed that he was involved in various criminal activities, too. Not only did he lack the credentials he professed, but he also never served as an adviser to any president as he claimed.

Despite widespread doubts about Napoleon Hill's credibility, his book sales continued to soar. "Think and Grow Rich" remains a significant commercial success even today. The principles outlined in this book, especially those related to positive thinking, laid the foundation for the modern self-help industry. Amid numerous allegations and criticisms, he is celebrated as one of the most influential motivational gurus.

Many of Hill's ideas were plagiarized in the widely acclaimed and bestselling book "The Secret." Hill has also ardently influenced figures like Tony Robbins. He has imparted his philosophies to notable personalities like Norman Vincent Peale and Donald Trump.

While Hill's Wikipedia page and official biographies portray him as a distinguished figure, his life was marked by deception and falsehoods. Police records indicate his involvement in numerous criminal activities and multiple arrests.

Hill's Wikipedia page often faces scrutiny from wiki moderators for appearing like an advertisement and lacking proper verification and citations. The allegations against him are substantiated by various authorities, and details are readily available in the public domain. However, the author of this book and the publisher do not intend to defame any individual.

Domains of the Self Help

Let's explore some of the primary domains in which self-help books and classes are prevalent:

- **Personality Development:** Personality development serves as a positive force for personal growth and self-improvement. It encourages individuals to work on themselves, identify areas for improvement, and develop new skills and habits that can benefit them in various aspects of life.
- **Spirituality:** Spirituality manifests in numerous forms, including non-religious spirituality led by figures like Sam Harris. This industry continues to flourish indefinitely.
- **Emotional Intelligence:** While emotional intelligence can be enhanced through practice, it requires rigorous ongoing training.
- **Time Management:** The effective utilization of time and resources concerns many individuals. Practical lessons addressing this issue should begin at a young age.

Other Main Topics Promoted by Self-Help Gurus are

- **Positive Thinking:** Embracing positive thoughts can help individuals overcome obstacles and attract more positivity and success into their lives. However, excessive positivity can be detrimental, a topic we'll explore in detail.
- **Goal Setting:** Establishing clear and attainable goals is crucial for personal and professional growth. Breaking significant goals into smaller steps maintains motivation and focus. However, fixating on one goal could result in a negative outcome.
- **Personal Responsibility:** Taking responsibility for actions and choices leads to personal growth. Learning from mistakes and making better decisions becomes possible. However, if not tackled properly, it could lead to self-blame and depression.
- **Cultivating Good Habits:** Nurturing positive habits results in lasting change and success. Replacing negative habits with positive ones enhances productivity and happiness.
- **Growth Mindset:** Believing in personal development through dedication and hard work empowers individuals to reach greater heights.
- **Time Management:** Effective time management ensures goal achievement and work-life balance. Prioritizing tasks, setting deadlines, and avoiding procrastination increase productivity and reduce stress.

- **Self-esteem and Confidence:** Building self-esteem and confidence enables individuals to face challenges, take risks, and achieve their goals.
- **Networking and Relationship Building:** Nurturing strong personal and professional relationships proves valuable throughout life.
- **Continuous Learning and Self-Improvement:** Lifelong learning and self-improvement aid in adapting to change, staying relevant in careers, and personal and professional growth.

Despite the undeniable value of these topics, the self-help industry thrives as a multimillion-dollar enterprise. How do motivational speakers attain celebrity status and charge exorbitant fees for sharing common knowledge easily accessible to everyone? Even though their one-man shows are often engaging and entertaining, the question arises: should we blindly follow what they preach? It's essential to critically evaluate the self-help industry's limitations and potential issues.

Where does it go wrong?

Let's critically and scientifically examine the shortcomings of the motivation industry:

- **Oversimplification:** Self-help materials often oversimplify complex problems with one-size-fits-all solutions that may not effectively address individual needs. Real-life challenges demand personalized and nuanced approaches tailored to unique circumstances.

- **Lack of Scientific Evidence:** Many self-help techniques lack empirical evidence and scientific research to support their claims, raising doubts about their effectiveness.
- **Quick Fixes:** The self-help industry may perpetuate the idea of instant transformation and quick fixes, fostering unrealistic expectations. Personal growth and development typically require time, effort, and patience.
- **Overemphasis on Personal Responsibility:** While personal responsibility is important, self-help resources sometimes place excessive emphasis on it, neglecting external factors like systemic barriers, socioeconomic conditions, and mental health issues that can impact one's journey.
- **Exploitation of Vulnerable Individuals:** Vulnerable individuals may turn to motivational gurus or self-help books in search of easy solutions, creating dependency on these resources when facing challenges.
- **Repetitive Content:** Repetition of similar messages and advice across many self-help resources can lead to redundancy and reduced impact.
- **Over commercialization:** The self-help industry has become a multibillion-dollar business, and some authors and speakers prioritize financial gain, raising questions about their genuine concern for the audience's well-being.
- **Lack of Professional Qualifications:** Most self-help writers and motivational speakers lack formal education, qualifications, or practical experience in psychology, counselling, or related fields, potentially limiting the depth of their expertise.

Unmasking Illusions and Realities

We hold no animosity towards any self-help promoters. It is undoubtedly a blessing for those who have found guidance and assistance in these books. Nevertheless, let's take a moment to reflect. Can we genuinely name a single remarkable individual who attained greatness solely by mastering and diligently following the shortcuts prescribed in self-improvement books?

The only way to accumulate wealth through self-help books is by writing and marketing one. The true beneficiaries of the self-improvement industry are its sellers. Ironically, those who purchase motivational books and frequently partake in such programs are the primary customers driving this industry.

So, where does it go wrong? These sellers claim to provide well-crafted business strategies catering to all behavioural patterns, offering ready-made interview skills and comprehensive practical formulas for every aspect of life. Unfortunately, they rely heavily on unscientific methods and pop psychological concepts like neuro-linguistic programming and transactional analysis. Often, they combine these pop psychological theories with oversimplified binary equations claimed to apply universally.

While aiming to offer customized solutions for achieving success in life, they occasionally descend into buffoonery.

3. Who Has The Key To Success?

What are the secrets to a successful life? If you ask this question, you will undoubtedly get ready-made answers like hard work, self-confidence, education, and intelligence. Each motivational guru will come up with freshly invented factors often cited as the formula for success. The interesting fact is that it's easy to spotlight these success elements in the lives of individuals like Steve Jobs, Bill Gates, and other notable figures. However, self-help experts conveniently overlook the fact that, much like any phenomenon in the universe, success is intricately connected to opportunities, evolution, and adaptation.

Nonetheless, it's important to note that some self-help authorities tend to disregard the crucial element that, just like any other phenomenon in the universe, the trajectory of success is intricately interwoven with several factors. Among these factors, the main important criterion is opportunities – favourable circumstances that allow growth and advancement. In the evolution of success, one may progressively change and refine one's strategies and approaches. Any successful person might have shown the ability to flexibly adjust to changing circumstances, a quality pivotal in the pursuit of success.

Since adaptation crucially determines the survival of organisms, the circumstances individuals encounter in life—whether adverse or favourable—along with their attitudes toward these circumstances, the decisions they make, the mental traits influencing those decisions, and the hereditary factors shaping them, and innumerable other known and unknown factors all play a pivotal role in defining the success of one's life.

In his book "Outliers," Canadian writer Malcolm Gladwell dissects the notion of success. He emphasizes that success is the result of accumulative advantages that happen in one's life. Moreover, he explains that these circumstances aren't always joyful. Sometimes these favourable factors could be traumatic or agonizing. In fact, famines, wars, conflicts, and diseases have frequently acted as unexpected catalysts for the success and fame of many remarkable individuals.

Exploring the Greatness of Gandhiji - A Multifaceted Analysis

Mohandas was born into a privileged and influential family in Gujarat. His father held the position of Diwan, or Chief Minister, in a princely state. During his youth, Mohandas never questioned the then prevalent practices such as child marriage, Sati, untouchability, and slavery. He never thought that British colonization was an evil. It can be inferred that he didn't express any objections to the actions of the British when he went to study in a country ruled by the very people who oppressed his own.

Upon reaching England, he even made many unsuccessful attempts to embrace British culture and lifestyle. In his quest to learn music, Gandhi struggled to attain proficiency despite his earnest efforts. Similarly, his endeavour to incorporate mutton into his diet failed due to his religious sentiments. Gandhi's bid to befriend a European girl in London also proved to be an utter failure. He also encountered challenges in his pursuit of learning dance, eventually abandoning it.

Gandhi pursued a law degree at the Inner Temple in London and achieved admission to the bar at the age of 22 in June 1891. So, what happened to his personality after that? How did Mohandas, a humble Indian young lawyer and admirer of the British, transform into a staunch opponent of the powerful British Empire? Let us delve into the transition of an ordinary Mohandas to one of the greatest personalities in the entire world. When we scientifically dissect and examine the happenings in the life of Gandhiji, we would derive newer insights.

On the one hand, despite being called to the bar in London, he couldn't argue in court, and he returned to India. His attempts to establish a law practice in Bombay faltered due to his psychological struggles with cross-examining witnesses. As a result, he settled in Rajkot, making a modest living by drafting petitions for litigants. He experienced two uncertain years in India.

In 1893, Gandhi received a legal assistance request from Dada Abdullah, a Muslim merchant from Kathiawar. Abdullah, who owned a prosperous shipping business in South Africa, required a lawyer for his distant cousin in Johannesburg. Gandhi inquired about the compensation, and they offered him a salary of £105 along with travel expenses. That was a good offer for Mohandas considering his current situation. Accepting the offer, Gandhi comprehended that it would entail a minimum one-year commitment in the Colony of Natal, South Africa, which was under British rule. In April 1893, at the age of 23, Gandhi sailed for South Africa to represent Abdullah's cousin. While he initially planned for a one-year stay, he ultimately spent a total of 21 years in South Africa.

It was in South Africa that Mohandas encountered the transformative circumstances instrumental in the transformation of this ordinary young man into a person admired by millions across the globe. Yes, it was during this time that he formulated his political ideologies, ethics, and activism.

One day, despite holding a first-class ticket, he was forcibly ejected from a train at night by a white man simply because an Indian was not deemed entitled to travel alongside white passengers in the first class. He was left alone the whole night in the lonely abandoned railway station. The emotional pain he endured, combined with his outrage at the oppression his people faced, ignited a sense of empathy, solidarity, and the courage to confront the powerful empire. This transformative encounter signified the emergence of Gandhiji, the revolutionary spirit that would mould his forthcoming journey.

Reverse your perspective

Without the emotional pain, outrage, and injustice he experienced on that fateful night, Gandhi might not have felt the profound sense of empathy and solidarity that became the driving force behind his activism. His time in South Africa, which was largely shaped by the discrimination and oppression he faced, might never have occurred. Gandhi may not have had the opportunity to formulate his political ideologies, ethics, and principles of nonviolent resistance.

Without these transformative experiences, Gandhi's life might have taken a more conventional path. He might have pursued a legal career, perhaps becoming a respected lawyer, but he may not have become the iconic figure and leader of the Indian independence movement that history remembers today.

The chance encounter with racial discrimination on that train in South Africa served as a catalyst, pushing Gandhi to become Gandhiji, the symbol of nonviolent resistance and civil rights. It set in motion a series of events that ultimately led to his pivotal role in India's struggle for independence. He could easily gain importance and acceptance in India, where the nationalist movement and struggle for independence were already gaining momentum.

So, in this alternate scenario, Gandhi's life may have lacked the extraordinary encounters and transformative instances that moulded his fate and shaped the course of history in a profound way. It underscores the role that chance, randomness, and unexpected events played in Gandhi's remarkable journey.

The Illusion of Glory and Success

When assessing individuals' achievements, it's crucial to avoid the misconception that greatness solely stems from adopting specific qualities or habits. It's more reasonable to recognize that exceptional individuals possess distinct habits.

Yet, even with this viewpoint, these habits are not the same for not even a dozen successful persons. Numerous successful people exhibit diverse habits.

To genuinely comprehend the success of remarkable individuals, examining their life circumstances and the advantages they received is vital. For instance, Albert Einstein's intellectual privilege significantly contributed to his success. However, it's important to highlight that his intellectual abilities flourished due to his escape from Nazi Jewish persecution and his refuge in America.

It is important to recognize that success is the result of a combination of diverse benefits that occur in one's life:

- Benefit of education and educational institutions: Many great people
- Benefit of wealth or poverty, wars or struggles: Many freedom fighters
- Benefit of the existing problem with the system: Karl Marx
- Benefit of health or disease: Helen Keller
- Benefit of technologies: Stephen Hawking

Moreover, it is worth remembering that success is not solely determined by these factors. Even if individuals like Hitler, Idi Amin, or Pol Pot were to be cloned and recreated, there would be no cause for fear. The circumstances that shaped them into who they were no longer exist, underscoring the complex nature of success and the multitude of factors involved. In a nutshell, it is the circumstances that mold an individual.

The Journey of the Majestic Giant Tree

Hyperion, located in California, stands as a remarkable coastal redwood, holding the esteemed title of being the world's tallest known living tree, reaching a breathtaking height of 115.92 meters (380.3 feet).

First Perspective: Observe this majestic tree, an embodiment of triumph. Despite facing numerous challenges throughout its growth, it never succumbed to adversity. With resolute determination, it weathered all unfavorable conditions, standing unwavering and stretching towards the heavens.

Second Perspective: In its youth, this tree remained untouched by animals, free from diseases, impervious to floods, strong winds, volcanic eruptions, and landslides. No woodcutter's axe ever fell upon it. There was a huge tree that prevented this sapling from getting enough sunlight. In every sense, it enjoyed unobstructed growth. Favourable conditions nurtured its progress, enabling it to flourish unhindered.

When highlighting a person's success, we have to look at both the resilience and the fortunate circumstances that propelled her to towering magnificence.

The Domino Effect

You might have heard that a small alteration within the Amazon Forest can significantly impact the Sahara Desert. Similarly, the Sahara Desert also influences the Amazon rainforest. This phenomenon is referred to as the "Domino Effect." The Domino Effect, known as the chain reaction or cascade effect, describes how a single event or a minute action triggers a chain of similar events or actions. It's often used metaphorically to illustrate how a minor initial incident can lead to major consequences.

Similarly, in our society and various sectors of life, a minor change in one area can catalyze significant changes in other parts, akin to a ripple effect. These changes could be physical, social, economic, or of any type. Even if these changes don't directly impact all aspects of life, they exert influence across various domains.

Whether referred to as the "Cascade Effect" or the "Snowball Effect," it signifies this process.

Here are some examples of the Domino Effect in our daily lives:

- A minor accident on a busy highway can slow down traffic, setting off a chain reaction of vehicles suddenly braking, leading to a traffic jam that affects miles of road behind the initial incident and causing many changes in the lives of those involved.
- Starting the day with a delay or being late for work due to a trivial reason can also trigger a series of delays in completing tasks. Yes, even this seemingly minute task can result in missed deadlines, stress, and a constant rushed feeling, or it can even alter the course of your career or life entirely.
- Sharing a thoughtless comment on social media can spark negative responses and arguments, potentially leading to online conflicts that escalate. This can have consequences such as job loss, legal repercussions, strained relationships, and even an impact on mental well-being.

Now, let's consider a more specific example. On a day of an extremely important exam or interview, you might experience a powerful headache. Even such a minor issue can prompt you to take a different path in your life. You may underperform in the interview, lose a promising job, and end up in a completely different field or area.

Inspirational literature often does not account for these complexities; it frequently offers binary solutions for everything. However, our world and our lives don't progress like a perfectly planned binary system.

The Pandemic's Silver Linings

If we look at a recent incident in history, COVID-19 has had the most widespread and impactful influence on the entire human race. It has caused trillions of dollars in global losses, deeply affecting countless lives. Many believed that life would never be the same again. However, amid these challenges, several industries experienced positive outcomes:

E-Commerce Companies: Lockdowns and regulations led to a significant increase in online shopping. E-commerce giants like Amazon, Flipkart, and Walmart-owned Flipkart saw substantial profits during the pandemic.

Video Conferencing Platforms: Remote work and virtual meetings became the norm, leading to remarkable growth in popularity and usage of video conferencing platforms like Zoom, Microsoft Teams, and Google Meet.

Streaming Services: With more people staying at home, streaming services like Netflix, Disney+ Hotstar, Apple TV+, and Amazon Prime Video gained widespread recognition during the lockdown and became part of daily routines.

Food Delivery Services: The closure of restaurants and the preference for home dining boosted the business of food delivery services like Swiggy and Zomato, providing a convenient alternative.

Telemedicine and Online Healthcare: The usage of telemedicine platforms and online healthcare services increased, with patients consulting doctors remotely, even from distant locations.

Online Education Platforms: The transition to remote learning for schools and colleges led to a surge in enrolment and usage of online education platforms.

Home Fitness Tools and Apps: With gym closures, there was a rise in demand for home fitness tools and apps.

Pharmaceutical Companies: Vaccine companies, mask and other durables manufacturing companies, COVID testing labs and lot of associated companies benefited a lot; the real advantages of which are known only to them.

Despite the challenges posed by the pandemic, millions of people directly benefited, either through increased profits or tangible advantages, during a time when the world was at a standstill due to this catastrophic event.

4. The Overemphasized Self-Confidence

Certain experts suggest that low self-confidence and a lack of self-worth play a significant role in children's mental health issues. They argue that family dynamics, including overindulgence or neglect, can lead to low self-esteem.

In the United States, some people link school shootings, especially those involving young individuals, to low self-esteem. However, scientific research doesn't strongly support this single theory because these issues have complex and varied underlying causes.

While psychology initially drew from philosophy, some still ground this field in philosophical and theological concepts. Some psychologists argue that the mind is separate from the body and influenced by external factors, refusing to accept the fact that humans are just another species and that the mind is the product of brain activity.

In our society, there's a common misconception that psychology is simply common sense. Many people believe that the essence of this science revolves around mind-reading, leading to statements like, "I know a bit of psychology."

Self-help experts and spiritual groups often emphasize the importance of self-esteem and self-empowerment in preventing mental health problems. For example, Nathaniel Branden, a self-help guru, highlights the role of self-esteem in mental well-being in his book "The 6 Pillars of Self-Esteem."

Now, let's scrutinize the arguments put forth by the

National Association for Self-Esteem. They assert that a lack of self-esteem is significantly linked to issues such as alcoholism, drug use, teenage pregnancy, school dropout, suicide, and learning disabilities. However, upon closer examination, we can establish that these claims lack substantial scientific support and remain unproven. Despite this debunking, many decision-makers, even in the government, continue to support the practice of giving over importance to self-esteem.

In 1986, the California state allocated an annual budget of $250,000 to an organization promoting self-esteem and social responsibility. The government also introduced incentives for school competitions to boost children's self-esteem.

In 2003, a group of psychologists, including Roy Baumeister, Jennifer Campbell, Kathleen Vaughn, Joe Kruger, and others, reviewed 15,000 studies on self-esteem and its relationship with mental health. They found a modest correlation between self-esteem and academic performance. However, it's crucial to understand that self-esteem alone doesn't significantly improve educational outcomes. Doing well academically may lead to high self-esteem, but having self-esteem doesn't automatically enhance academic achievements. It's essential to recognize that the notion that low self-confidence is directly correlated to depression is also not substantiated by any scientific evidence (Baumeister et al., 2003; Meier, 2010).

Relationship Between Aggression and Self-Esteem:

There is a widespread notion that people with low self-esteem indulge in more violent behavior. However, studies have disproved that. On the contrary there are evidence to establish that individuals with high self-esteem can sometimes exhibit increased aggression. These people often possess a sense of entitlement, believing they deserve special treatment and are superior to others. When their confidence, authority, importance, or status is challenged, they may respond with strong anger and aggression.

Self-Serving Bias:

Throughout the history of psychology, there has been a prevailing belief in society that many individuals lack genuine confidence in their abilities. It's commonly assumed that feelings of inferiority, self-disdain, and a lack of self-appreciation are widespread among people. However, in the past five decades, extensive research conducted by social psychologists across different societies has challenged and disproven this notion.

In reality, every human being tends to perceive themselves as distinct and special compared to others. This type of thinking can actually be advantageous. Our self-esteem, to some extent, operates as an illusion, and this illusion plays a crucial role in motivating us on a biological level.

Imagine a scenario where we continually assess ourselves critically and realistically.

Here, we focus solely on our failures, shortcomings, and faults. You would indeed feel very inferior and incompatible compared to your peers. Such an approach would be detrimental to our overall well-being. Acknowledging the reality of our imperfections could potentially lead to a loss of confidence, increased fear, and even mental exhaustion. However, over the course of our evolutionary history, we have developed some strong psychological defense mechanisms that counteract these negative effects. These mechanisms help us cope with the fear of self-doubt and enable us to confront reality more effectively.

One common example of self-serving bias is when a student performs well on an exam and attributes their success to their intelligence and hard work. On the other hand, if the student performs poorly, they may attribute it to factors like a difficult test or distractions in the environment.

In the realm of self-help, self-serving bias is often utilized to promote personal development and motivation.

Many self-help books and programs encourage individuals to adopt a positive mindset and take credit for their successes, thus boosting self-confidence and fostering a belief in one's abilities.

For instance, a self-help book might encourage readers to view setbacks as temporary and external factors, while emphasizing their own skills and determination as the driving force behind their achievements. By framing failures as external and successes as internal, self-help resources aim to motivate individuals to persist in their goals and take proactive steps towards self-improvement.

But even then, occasionally, we experience moments of realism where we gain a clearer understanding of our real self and self-worth. During these times, our self-assurance might waver, and we may feel a heightened sense of anxiety and disappointment. Previous failures and setbacks might come as an avalanche to our memory, leaving us disheartened. But this is temporary and short-lasting. In response, our psychological defences kick in, allowing us to quickly regain our inner strength and resilience. However, it's crucial to exercise caution when it comes to excessively overestimating our abilities, as this can become problematic beyond a certain threshold.

5. Each Man Is Not An Island

I am a superman

Research has shown that individuals tend to have distorted perceptions of both success and failure. Successes are often attributed to one's personal talents and diligent efforts, while failures are commonly attributed to external factors such as bad luck, conspiracies, flawed systems, or the actions of others.

As we age, we may start attributing past failures to other people or external circumstances. This tendency becomes more prominent when we compare ourselves to others and evaluate our own capabilities. For instance, we might believe that we are better drivers, more responsible children, deeper thinkers, younger at heart, more affectionate partners, or even longer-lived than our peers.

If you're currently reading this and find yourself thinking that you don't fit into this category, it might indicate that your self-assessment is not entirely accurate. Let's delve deeper into these aspects of yourself.

Home Schooling fad

I've heard parents discuss their decision to homeschool their child, a choice that's gaining popularity now a days. When one of my clients revealed her decision to homeschool her child, I shared my thoughts with her:

"I understand that you might not take my advice into account. Nevertheless, as both a human being and a psychologist, I feel morally obligated to say this: You're potentially causing significant harm to your child."

As expected, my words did not have much impact on her, and I chose not to continue the conversation.

Drawbacks of Homeschooling

If your main focus is academics, homeschooling might not seem much problematic. It is because nowadays, online learning offers several advantages, often surpassing traditional schools in terms of quality and cost. We can choose the time, teachers, medium, pace, and many more things at the convenience of our home. We indeed could opt for better quality learning and information than traditional schooling. But there lies a problem.

The 360-degree Learning Phase

During my stint at the Indian Institute of Management Kozhikode, I have heard students open up about the real benefits of graduating from top-notch business schools. In their own words: "Our success doesn't come from learning anything extraordinary at institutes like IIMs, XLRI, or ISB. We don't learn any hidden secrets of business from these schools. It's the institution's reputation and brand name that give us an advantage. Moreover, we get to know many people in the industry, and we get associated with a good peer network that can help us later."

Evolution shaped us as social beings, and homeschooling can disrupt these essential connections. Children need to learn soft skills like patience, empathy, friendship, and communication skills. They should engage in physical activities and experiment with many other things with their peers. They must grasp the emotions of the opposite gender and navigate the psychological and physical changes appropriate for their age.

Let us look at the drawbacks of home schooling

Socialization: Homeschooled children may not have as many opportunities to interact with peers of different ages, backgrounds, and personalities, which can impact their ability to form friendships, navigate social situations, and develop emotional intelligence.

Conflict resolution: Home-schooling may limit children's opportunities to practice conflict resolution skills, such as negotiating, compromising, and resolving disagreements with peers.

Emotional regulation: Homeschooled children may not have as many opportunities to practice emotional regulation skills, such as managing frustration, anger, and anxiety, in a group setting.

Empathy: Home-schooling may limit children's opportunities to develop empathy by interacting with peers who may have different perspectives, experiences, and emotions.

Self-awareness: Homeschooled children may not have as many opportunities to develop self-awareness skills, such as recognizing their strengths and weaknesses, and understanding their emotions and motivations.

Self-advocacy: Homeschooling may limit children's opportunities to practice self-advocacy skills, such as communicating their needs and preferences, and standing up for themselves in a respectful manner.

Teamwork: Homeschooled children may not have as many opportunities to work in teams, which can impact their ability to collaborate, delegate tasks, and build on others' ideas.

Leadership: Homeschooling may limit children's opportunities to develop leadership skills, such as taking charge of a group project, leading a discussion, or mentoring a younger child.

Communication: Homeschooled children may not have as many opportunities to practice communication skills, such as public speaking, presenting ideas, and negotiating with others.

Adaptability: Homeschooling may limit children's opportunities to develop adaptability skills, such as adjusting to new situations, coping with unexpected changes, and being open to new experiences.

Homeschooling might lead to a lack of motivation to excel in a competitive environment and the acquisition of essential social skills. Most importantly, homeschooling poses challenges for parents. It consumes parents' time, narrows their focus on their child's academics, and diminishes physical exercise and mental engagement. The pressure on families can make life challenging for both homeschooled children and parents.

The Self-Made Aliens

Many people boast that they are a self-made person. The term "self-made" typically implies that one's accomplishments are solely the result of their own hard work and determination. This perspective suggests that an individual's path to success is entirely self-reliant, with no significant external influences. However, this perspective fails to consider the profound impact of one's surroundings on them and the support of others he/she received.

To illustrate this interconnectedness, consider the various stages of life. From the moment of birth, we are entirely dependent on our parents and caregivers for survival. This dependency continues as we grow and enter the educational system, where teachers and mentors provide guidance, knowledge, and support. The friends and acquaintances we make throughout our lives also contribute significantly to our personal and professional growth.

Furthermore, the technological advancements that enable us to lead more efficient lives are the result of the collaborative efforts of millions of people around the world. The smartphone in our hands, for instance, is not the creation of a single individual but a product of the collective work of countless engineers, designers, manufacturers, and innumerable others.

The success of any individual is undeniably influenced by various factors, including individual talents, hard work, and the opportunities that come one's way. However, it is equally important to acknowledge the role of the people we interact with daily. Our peers, colleagues, and social networks all play a pivotal role in shaping our achievements.

By understanding that no one is truly self-made, we can work towards building a more inclusive and supportive society where everyone has the opportunity to thrive and succeed.

6. The Self-Help Industry And Psychological Theories

Within the realm of self-help literature, motivational seminars, and personality development training, a multitude of psychological theories are frequently and widely used. What makes this field intriguing is that every motivational guru and self-help author often presents new psychological theories, acting as both creators and practitioners of these concepts. However, it's crucial to note that these theories are often rooted in the personalities and imaginations of these motivational figures and typically lack any scientific substantiation.

Unfortunately, over time, some of these theories are presented as genuine psychology and may even gain popularity as therapeutic techniques. A notable example of this phenomenon can be observed in the cases of transactional analysis and neuro-linguistic programming.

It is vital to acknowledge that the theories and seminars on motivation and self-help are heavily affected by cognitive biases and logical fallacies. This can impact the accuracy and reliability of the programs they offer. These pop psychological theories are widely practiced and followed much more than scientific psychological theories. Let us have a look at the cognitive biases and logical fallacies widely practiced within these self-help industries.

Cognitive Bias

Cognitive biases are systematic patterns in our thinking that cause us to deviate from rational decision-making. These biases stem from our mental processes and can lead to distortions in our perceptions, reasoning, and choices. They often operate without our conscious awareness and can result in incorrect or flawed conclusions. Recognizing these biases is crucial, as they can impact various aspects of life, from personal decisions to professional choices. Understanding these biases enables us to make better and more objective decisions.

Logical Fallacies

A logical fallacy is a mistake in reasoning that renders an argument invalid. It can lead to incorrect or deceptive conclusions. Logical fallacies may be persuasive on the surface, but they lack sound and valid reasoning. Recognizing logical fallacies is essential for fostering critical thinking and making well-informed decisions.

1. The Sunk Cost Fallacy

The sunk cost fallacy refers to the inclination to continue in a situation or pursuit, even when it is detrimental, only because of the fact that you have spent a lot of o the resources, such as time, effort, or money, already in it.

Consider this scenario: You've purchased tickets for a movie, but on the day of your planned outing, you catch a cold. Fearing the potential loss of money, you decide to go to the movies. In this situation, despite not being able to fully enjoy the movie, you might worsen your illness and potentially spread it to others. Furthermore, you could end up missing two days of work income.

Sometimes, people order excessive amounts of food and overeat in an attempt to make use of their money. It's wiser to stop eating when you feel satisfied, as overeating can negatively affect your health. Similarly, if you're watching a movie and find it boring, it's a fallacy to think you have to continue watching it just because you've started it. If you don't like the movie, it's perfectly fine to stop watching. By doing so, you save your time, energy, and avoid unnecessary frustration.

In situations where a couple realizes they are incompatible and cannot live together, it's best to end the relationship. Likewise, when you find yourself losing an argument, it's often better to gracefully let it go and move on. People sometimes fall into the trap of investing more time and money in a venture, even when it's evident that it won't be successful. They do this in the hope of recouping their losses, but such thinking can lead to financial disasters.

We've all heard inspiring stories of individuals who persisted until the end and ultimately succeeded. Phrases like "never give up" and "hold on until the end" are often preached by motivational speakers. However, it's important to remember that we only hear about the success stories of those who persisted until the end and achieved success. We never hear about people who faced significant setbacks and saved their lives because they decided to stop along the way. Nor do we hear about those who, despite having the opportunity to stop and escape, continued forward and ultimately suffered breakdowns due to the illogical belief that everything would turn out okay.

2. Bandwagon Effect

The bandwagon effect is a cognitive bias in which people tend to adopt certain behaviors, beliefs, or trends because they see others doing the same. Essentially, it's the "jump on the bandwagon" mentality where people want to be part of something that's popular, assuming that if so many others are doing it, it must be worthwhile.

When people see a self-help trend gaining momentum and a significant following, they are more likely to believe in its effectiveness and join the movement.

The Psychology of the Bandwagon Effect in Self-Help

- **Validation:** Humans are social creatures. We seek validation from others, and we often gauge the validity of an idea or movement based on how many others are endorsing it. In the self-help industry, when individuals observe the growing popularity of a particular method or approach, they are more likely to view it as legitimate and effective.
- **Fear of Missing Out (FOMO):** The fear of missing out is a powerful motivator. When people see that many are benefiting from a self-help trend, they don't want to be left behind. They fear missing out on the potential life-changing benefits that others seem to be experiencing.
- **Social Proof:** This phenomenon, closely related to the bandwagon effect, is when individuals look to others for

guidance on how to behave in ambiguous situations. In the self-help context, seeing countless testimonials and success stories reinforces the belief that a particular method works and can genuinely help.

Examples of the Bandwagon Effect in Self-Help

- **Positive Affirmations:** Positive affirmations, where individuals repeat positive statements to boost self-esteem, are widely popular in self-help. When people see friends, celebrities, or influential figures endorsing the practice and sharing their experiences, they are more likely to start using affirmations themselves.
- **Mindfulness and Meditation:** The rising popularity of mindfulness and meditation is partially due to the bandwagon effect. As these practices gained traction in popular culture and media, more people jumped on board, believing that they, too, could achieve mental well-being and personal growth.
- **Life Coaching:** Life coaching, once considered unconventional, has become a booming industry. The bandwagon effect plays a substantial role here as people see others seeking guidance and support from life coaches, which encourages them to follow suit.

The bandwagon effect can also lead to uncritical acceptance and the perpetuation of fads and pseudoscience. The self-help industry is not immune to dubious practices, and many people may fall victim to unverified or unhelpful trends simply because they're in vogue.

3. Illusory correlation

Illusory correlation is a cognitive bias that refers to the tendency for people to perceive a correlation or relationship between two things when there is none. This bias can be particularly problematic in the self-help industry, where many products and services are marketed as having the ability to solve a wide range of problems.

Here are some ways in which illusory correlation can manifest in the self-help industry:

- **False Promises:** Many self-help products and services promise unrealistic results, such as guaranteed weight loss, improved relationships, or increased success. These promises are often based on anecdotal evidence or testimonials rather than scientific research. As a result, consumers may feel that they have found a solution to their problems when, in reality, there is no scientific evidence to support the claims.
- **Placebo Effect:** Consumers may experience improvements in their health or well-being as a result of their belief in a treatment, rather than the treatment itself. The self-help industry often exploits the placebo effect by marketing products and services as having the ability to solve a wide range of problems, even if there is no scientific evidence to support the claims.
- **Selection Bias:** Self-help products and services often selectively choose testimonials and success stories that support their claims, while ignoring those that do not. This

can create the illusion that the product or service is more effective than it actually is.

- **Correlation vs. Causation:** Self-help products and services often claim that certain behaviors or practices are the cause of success, when in reality, they may just be correlated with success. For example, a self-help book may claim that visualizing success is the key to achieving it, when in reality, there are many other factors that contribute to success.
- **Cherry Picking:** Self-help products and services often cherry-pick the research that supports their claims, while ignoring research that contradicts them. This can create the illusion that the product or service is supported by scientific evidence when, in reality, the evidence is mixed or non-existent.
- **Misuse of Statistics:** Self-help products and services often use statistics in a misleading way, such as by citing isolated studies or using data out of context. This can create the illusion that the product or service is more effective than it actually is.

4. Confirmation bias

Where do your beliefs and opinions come from? Many people assume that their beliefs are rational and neutral. They often think their opinions and judgments stem from their years of experience and careful analysis .They are sure that they are more logical than others' thoughts.

The truth is that we are all susceptible to a subtle problem known as confirmation bias. We tend to seek and accept only the information that aligns with our existing beliefs, while ignoring information that challenges our beliefs.

Here are some ways in which confirmation bias can manifest in the context of self-help:

- **Selective Reading:** Individuals may choose to read self-help books, articles, or social media posts that confirm their existing beliefs while dismissing information that contradicts their beliefs. People may actively look for self-help resources that align with their current beliefs, such as a book that reinforces their belief in their ability to achieve a specific goal.
- **Biased Interpretation:** People are more likely to accept and internalize self-help information that confirms their existing beliefs while rejecting information that contradicts them.
- **Overconfidence:** Confirmation bias can lead to overconfidence in one's abilities, as people selectively focus on information that confirms their strengths and neglect information that reveals their weaknesses.
- **Lack of Self-Awareness:** Confirmation bias can reduce self-awareness as individuals are less likely to seek or acknowledge information that contradicts their beliefs about themselves.
- **Difficulty in Changing Beliefs:** It can be challenging for people to change their beliefs due to confirmation bias, as they may resist information that contradicts their existing beliefs. It can hinder individuals from recognizing their own limitations, as they tend to focus on information that confirms their beliefs about their abilities.

To avoid the pitfalls of confirmation bias in self-help, it's crucial to be aware of this bias and actively seek out diverse perspectives and information that challenge your beliefs.

5. Illusory Truth Effect

The Illusory Truth Effect is a psychological phenomenon where people tend to believe information that is repeated frequently, even if it is not true. This can be particularly problematic in the context of self-help, where individuals in pursuit of improving their lives may be more susceptible to false or misleading information. Here are some ways in which the Illusory Truth Effect can manifest in the context of self-help:

- **False or Misleading Information:** Self-help books, articles, and social media posts may contain false or misleading information that is repeated frequently, such as the idea that visualization can solve all problems or that positive thinking can cure illnesses.
- **Repetition of Affirmations:** Affirmations are positive statements that individuals may repeat to themselves to reprogram their minds and change their beliefs. However, repetition of affirmations can also contribute to the Illusory Truth Effect, as individuals may start to believe the affirmations even if they are not based on reality.
- **Testimonials:** Self-help resources often include testimonials from individuals who have achieved success or overcome challenges using the techniques presented. However, these testimonials may be anecdotal, paid or advertisements and not representative of the average

person's experience. This may lead to an illusory belief in the effectiveness of the techniques.

- **Charismatic Leaders:** Some self-help leaders may have a charismatic presence and can persuade their followers to believe in their ideas, even if those ideas lack a basis in evidence.
- **Groupthink:** Self-help groups and communities may reinforce certain beliefs and ideas, leading to a groupthink effect where individuals believe information that is not supported by evidence.
- **Lack of Critical Thinking:** Self-help resources may encourage individuals to accept their ideas without questioning or critically evaluating them.
- **Emotional Appeal:** Self-help resources may appeal to individuals' emotions by using stories or anecdotes that evoke feelings like hope, excitement, or fear. This emotional appeal can make individuals more susceptible to believing information not supported by evidence.

To illustrate the potential consequences, let's consider the tactics used by Joseph Goebbels, Nazi Germany's Minister of Propaganda, who applied specific rules: 'Never allow the public to become emotionally cold, never admit any wrongdoing on our part, never assume that there is any good in the enemy, never give any room for alternative thoughts, never blame yourself, focus on one enemy at a time, and blame him for everything that happens around him. People will definitely believe you.'

Ultimately, even if we were initially convinced that a piece of information is false, this illusion can come back to haunt us.

6. Illusion of Justice

The Illusion of Justice is a psychological phenomenon where people tend to believe that they have more control over events than they actually do. This can be particularly problematic in the context of self-help, where individuals may think they possess the power to change their lives and achieve their goals through sheer willpower and determination.

Here are some ways in which the Illusion of Justice can manifest in the context of self-help:

- **Overestimation of Personal Control:** Self-help resources may encourage individuals to believe that they have more control over their lives and circumstances than they actually do. This can lead to unrealistic expectations and disappointment when things do not go as planned.
- **Underestimation of External Factors:** Self-help resources may downplay the impact of external factors, such as luck, privilege, or systemic injustices, on an individual's success or failure. This can lead to a false belief that success is solely the result of personal effort and that failure is due to personal shortcomings.
- **Overemphasis on Personal Responsibility:** The motivational industry often overemphasizes the importance of personal responsibility, leading individuals to believe that they are solely responsible for their success or failure. This can lead to feelings of guilt, shame, or inadequacy when things don't go as planned. It may also ignore or downplay the impact of structural barriers, such as racism, sexism, or ableism, on an individual's ability to succeed. This can lead

to a false belief that success is equally accessible to everyone, regardless of their background or identity.

- **Over Reliance on Individual Effort:** Self-help resources may encourage individuals to rely solely on their own effort and willpower to achieve their goals. This can lead to a lack of recognition of the importance of external factors, such as opportunity, resources, and support, in achieving success. They conveniently ignore the role of privilege in an individual's success or failure. This can lead to a false belief that success is solely the result of personal effort and that anyone can achieve success if they work hard enough. The role of systemic injustices, such as discrimination, inequality, and oppression, in an individual's success or failure are not at all taken into consideration here. This can lead to a false belief that success is solely the result of personal effort and that anyone can achieve success if they work hard enough.

7. The just-world phenomenon

The just-world phenomenon refers to the belief that this world is inherently just, and therefore, our actions and moral conduct determine our outcomes. This perspective leads us to believe that those who do good will be rewarded, while those who do wrong will be punished. People have a natural inclination to want to believe that the world is fair and just. So whenever they witness an injustice, they often seek ways to justify, explain, or rationalize it.

Here are some ways in which the just-world phenomenon can manifest in the context of self-help:

- **Victim-Blaming:** Self-help resources may encourage individuals to take responsibility for their own problems, which can be empowering indeed. However, they may also perpetuate the idea that individuals are entirely responsible for their circumstances, potentially leading to victim-blaming. Individuals are seen as at fault for their own problems, rather than recognizing the role of external factors.
- **Overemphasis on Personal Responsibility:** Self-help resources may place excessive emphasis on personal responsibility, leading individuals to believe they have complete control over their lives and circumstances. This can be detrimental as it overlooks the impact of external factors, such as systemic injustices, privilege, and oppression. They may ignore or downplay the impact of structural barriers, such as racism, sexism, and ableism, on an individual's ability to succeed. This can foster a false belief that success is equally accessible to everyone, regardless of their background or identity. Self-help resources may encourage individuals to focus solely on their own effort and willpower, rather than recognizing the importance of external factors like opportunity, resources, and support. This can lead to the belief that success is solely the result of individual effort, neglecting the role of privilege and opportunity.

Why does the just-world phenomenon occur?

People never like to think that they will ever be the victim of a violent crime. Therefore, when hearing about an incident such as assault or rape, people may try to blame the victim's behaviour, such as their dressing, careless behaviour, or dressing styles. Additionally, people often view nature as a benevolent force and find it challenging to accept that it can cause harm to living beings. This phenomenon offers a sense of control by attributing individual responsibility for personal misfortunes.

8. Optimism bias

Optimism bias is the tendency to overestimate the likelihood of positive events in our lives and underestimate the likelihood of negative events. We agree that a touch of optimism is essential all the time. It can inspire perseverance in the face of difficulties and rejections. However, it could also lead us astray by blinding us to potential downsides and resulting in poor decision-making. As humans, we consider ourselves rational beings, but in reality, we may often overestimate positive events and be overly optimistic leading us to danger.

Optimism bias manifests as the false belief that we are more likely to experience positive events in our lives than others and less likely to encounter undesirable ones. In essence, we overestimate the probability of positive or happy events occurring, potentially leading to misguided life choices.

Here are some ways in which optimism bias can manifest in self-help:

- **Unrealistic Expectations:** Self-help resources may foster unrealistic expectations about what can be achieved through personal effort and hard work, which can result in disappointment and frustration when these expectations are not met. They may encourage individuals to believe they have more control over their lives and circumstances than they actually do, leading to a false sense of security and a lack of preparedness for unexpected events.
- **Underestimation of Obstacles:** Self-help resources may downplay the obstacles and challenges individuals may face in their pursuit of personal growth and achievement, potentially resulting in inadequate planning and preparation for potential roadblocks.
- **Overemphasis on Positive Thinking:** They may excessively emphasize the importance of positive thinking and a positive attitude. While a positive attitude can be beneficial, it is not a guaranteed path to success and can divert attention from the need for practical action and planning.

9. Magical thinking

Magical thinking is a common phenomenon in the self-help industry, where individuals may believe that certain actions or practices can bring about desired outcomes without any logical or scientific basis. This can include beliefs in the power of positive thinking, the law of attraction, or the idea that one's thoughts and beliefs can shape their reality.

Here are some ways in which magical thinking may manifest in the self-help industry:

- **Law of Attraction:** This belief suggests that one's thoughts, whether positive or negative, can attract corresponding events into their life. It operates on the premise that the universe responds to one's thoughts.
- **Manifestation:** This idea centers on the power of visualization and intention-setting to bring about desired outcomes, sometimes without the need for concrete actions.
- **Crystals and Energy:** Some individuals turn to crystals and energy healing, despite a lack of scientific backing, to promote well-being or success.
- **Superstitions:** Superstitions, like lucky charms or rituals, may be incorporated into personal development or goal achievement, despite their irrational nature.
- **Magical Rituals:** Individuals engage in ceremonies, spells, or rituals rooted in esoteric or mystical traditions to influence life circumstances.
- **Psychic or Astrological Guidance:** Some seek advice and decision-making from astrologers, psychics, or mediums regarding life and future events.

These practices are prevalent in the self-help industry, where some believe in the power of thoughts, affirmations, and mindset to bring about tangible results, such as success, weight loss, or personal transformation. While these ideas can be motivating and empowering, they may also overlook the role of practical actions, external factors, privilege, and systemic injustices in shaping one's life.

10. Control Bias

Control bias refers to our tendency to overestimate the degree of control we have over our emotional behaviours. Self-help asserts the power of willpower, and many believe that we have a lot of control over our "internal urges" such as hunger, drug addiction, fatigue, or sexual arousal.

The Kellogg School of Management in Chicago conducted a study on "control bias." They found that as independent individuals we have no idea how much temptation we can withstand. The study found that people who were less confident about their ability to resist temptation performed better in a test to resist temptation. They did it because they kept the source of temptation as far away as possible.

Self-control bias is widely used in self-help and personal development literature, as it can motivate individuals to take action and make positive changes in their lives. However, it's important to recognize that self-control bias can also lead to negative consequences, such as:

- **Overestimation of abilities:** Individuals may overestimate their ability to control events or outcomes, leading to disappointment or frustration when they are unable to achieve their goals.
- **Lack of preparedness:** Self-control bias can lead individuals to underestimate the role of chance or external factors in their lives, leaving them unprepared for unexpected events or challenges.
- **Increased stress and anxiety:** The pressure to control events or outcomes can lead to increased stress and anxiety,

particularly when individuals are unable to achieve their goals.

To avoid the negative consequences of self-control bias, it's important to cultivate a realistic understanding of one's control and recognize the limits of one's abilities. This can involve:

- Recognize that some events or outcomes are outside of your control and that chance or external factors can play a significant role in their occurrence.
- Set goals that are within your control and that are not dependent on external factors.

Overall, self-control bias can be a useful tool for motivation and personal growth, but it's important to use it in moderation and to recognize its limitations. By cultivating a realistic understanding of one's control and recognizing the role of chance and external factors, individuals can avoid the negative consequences of self-control bias and achieve their goals in a healthy and balanced way.

11. Survivorship Bias

Survival bias is a common perceptual error that distorts our understanding of the world. Every day we hear the stories of many successful people. But we don't pay enough attention to the past failures of these same successful people.

For every great success in the world, there are thousands of failures to tell. But stories of failures are not as compelling as stories of success. So, they are rarely spoken or written. As we repeat every success story, we forget the real statistics of success and failure and overestimate the chances of success in life.

Let's look at one of the most famous examples of survivorship bias. During the time of World War II, the US military asked the great mathematician Abraham Wald to study how to protect aircrafts from being shot down. They initially were in the practice of inspecting the aircrafts returning from combat without major injuries, analyzing where they were hit the worst, and then reinforcing those areas.

However, Wald realized that they were making a big mistake in their analysis. They were falling victim to survivorship bias. In reality, they were supposed to be inspecting crashed planes. They were to learn and inspect why they broke, and the reasons were to be analysed.

This fallacy or bias is most often used by motivational gurus and self-help books. When we only focus only on successful people in life, we suffer from survivorship bias. Often our attention is drawn to people who take risks and succeed despite problems.

For example, we might have heard it many times that many of today's billionaires including Bill Gates and Mark Zuckerberg did not complete their university studies. Yet they have achieved success. This information attracted considerable media attention. The New York Times later reported that the number of young people who decided not to go to university increased a lot after this.

In 2011, Silicon Valley entrepreneur Peter Thiel launched a new program. He promised an award of $100,000 to young entrepreneurs who wanted to drop out of school and start a new business. The outcome of this program proved to be detrimental. The future of many people has been ruined only because of this. No one bothered to report the information of thousands of people who dropped out of university and became a huge failure in life. Yes, this news is not worth selling because nobody wants to hear the story of failure or the stories of realities.

12. The Illusion of Transparency

The Illusion of Transparency is a cognitive bias that refers to the tendency for people to overestimate the degree to which others can understand their thoughts, feelings, and intentions. This bias can lead individuals to believe that they are being more transparent and open than they actually are, and that others can easily understand their perspective.

Here are a few examples of the Illusion of Transparency:

A person thinks that their facial expressions and body language clearly convey their emotions and intentions, but in reality, others may not be able to read their emotions accurately.

A person believes that their words and actions are clear and straightforward, but others may misinterpret them due to different perspectives or misunderstandings.

A person assumes that their friends and family members understand their thoughts and feelings without needing to be told, but in reality, they may not be aware of the person's inner experiences.

The Illusion of Transparency is widely used in self-help and personal development literature, as it can motivate individuals to communicate more effectively and build stronger relationships. However, it's important to recognize that the Illusion of Transparency can also have negative consequences, such as:

- **Miscommunication:** The Illusion of Transparency can lead to miscommunication, as individuals may assume that others understand their perspective when in fact they do not.
- **Misinterpretation:** The Illusion of Transparency can also lead to misinterpretation, as others may interpret an individual's words and actions in a way that is different from what was intended.
- **Relationship conflicts:** The Illusion of Transparency can lead to conflicts in relationships, as individuals may assume that their partner or friends understand their thoughts and feelings when in fact they do not.

To avoid the negative consequences of the Illusion of Transparency, it's important to cultivate effective communication skills and recognize the limits of one's transparency. This can involve:

- Listen carefully to others and ask questions to ensure that you understand their perspective accurately. Use clear and concise language to express your thoughts and feelings, and avoid making assumptions about others' understanding.
- Ask for feedback from others to ensure that your communication is effective and that they understand your perspective accurately.

13. Selective Perception Bias

Suppose two people see the same thing at the same time. Even if the visual signals that fall on their eyes are the same, their analysis will be of two types. This is called perception. Individuals' attitudes, life circumstances, interests, repressed emotions, social, educational, and cultural circumstances etc. will all significantly influence their perceptions. Things that do not come under the scope of our desires, interests, etc. would be peeled away. Selective perception is when we pick up only a few sentences that we want from an ocean of information.

Selective perception is the process of picking out and accepting only those things from a speech, book, or news that they feel are true. We take only what we need, completely ignoring opposing views. In other words, a person sees only what she wants to see in an image. No one sees the real picture.

All people tend to 'see things' based on their own particular frame of reference. We interpret all information only in ways that are consistent with our existing values and beliefs. Psychologists say that this process happens unconsciously.

Here are some examples of Selective Perception Bias in the self-help industry:

1. Confirmation bias in goal setting: Individuals may set goals that are aligned with their existing beliefs and values, and selectively seek out information that confirms their ability to achieve those goals. For example, someone who wants to start a successful business may selectively seek out stories of successful entrepreneurs who started their businesses in similar circumstances, while ignoring stories of entrepreneurs who failed.

2. **Selective attention to positive feedback:** Individuals may selectively focus on positive feedback and ignore negative feedback. For example, someone who is trying to improve their public speaking skills may selectively focus on positive feedback from friends and family, while ignoring constructive criticism from others.

3. **Biased interpretation of information**: Individuals may interpret information in a biased way that confirms their existing beliefs. For example, someone who believes that they are not good at public speaking may interpret feedback from a speech as evidence that they are not good enough, while ignoring feedback that suggests otherwise. Someone who believes that a certain self-help technique is effective may selectively seek out studies that support that belief, while ignoring studies that suggest otherwise.

4. **Selective exposure to information:** Individuals may selectively expose themselves to information that confirms their existing beliefs and avoid information that contradicts them. For example, someone who wants to improve their communication skills may selectively seek out books and articles that confirm their existing beliefs about communication, while avoiding books and articles that present alternative perspectives.

5. **Selective use of anecdotal evidence:** Individuals may selectively use anecdotal evidence to support their existing beliefs, while ignoring contradictory evidence. For example, someone who believes that a certain self-help technique is

effective may selectively share anecdotes about people who have successfully used the technique, while ignoring anecdotes about people who have not had success with the technique.

Let's explore another intriguing example: On the occasion of a bishop's visit to the seminary, he delivered a speech to its clergy students. While discussing the glory of motherhood, he quoted a statement by Pandit Nehru: "Our first prime minister, Pandit Jawaharlal Nehru, once said, 'I have felt the greatest satisfaction when I slept on the lap of someone else's wife. That woman was none other than my own father's wife. I got the greatest solace of my life on my mother's lap.'"

The audience comprised seminary students in their late adolescence and early youth. One of them had the opportunity to preach in a parish after two weeks. This is how he conveyed the lines from the bishop's speech at the seminary: "I will tell you the truth, my dear parishioners. The greatest satisfaction I ever had was when I slept on the lap of another man's wife." In reality, during the bishop's speech, this clergy student didn't pay much attention to what was said before and after this sentence.

The believers were disturbed upon hearing this sentence. Seeing that things were escalating, the aspirant priest intervened, saying, "Don't be upset by this. Not only I, but our bishop has also had similar experiences

14. Baader-Meinhof Phenomenon

The Baader-Meinhof Phenomenon, also known as the frequency illusion or the recency illusion, is a psychological phenomenon where a person notices a word, phrase, or concept, and then suddenly begins seeing it everywhere. This can happen in various contexts, including the self-help industry. For example, you are thinking of buying a Tata Nexon car. After that you start noticing its advertisements in many places. You understand that there is a lot of this vehicle on the road. It is actually a game of your brain. All these ads and this vehicle have been there before.

In the self-help industry, the Baader-Meinhof Phenomenon can manifest in several ways. For example:

1. Self-help jargon: Self-help books, seminars, and social media often use a specific set of buzzwords and phrases that become popular and trendy. Once a person becomes familiar with these terms, they may start noticing them everywhere, even in places where they were not previously aware of them.

2. Social influence: Social media platforms, in particular, can contribute to the Baader-Meinhof Phenomenon. When people see their friends and influencers sharing self-help content, they may start noticing it more frequently and feel like it's everywhere.

3. Personal growth: When people are in the process of personal growth and self-improvement, they may become more aware of self-help concepts and phrases. This increased awareness can lead to the illusion that these concepts and phrases are popping up everywhere.

It's important to note that the Baader-Meinhof Phenomenon is a subjective experience and not a reflection of the actual frequency of the word or concept. It's a psychological response to the way our brains process information and can be influenced by various factors.

15. The Pygmalion effect

The Pygmalion effect is a psychological phenomenon that occurs when a person's beliefs and expectations about their own abilities and behavior influence their performance and behavior. In the context of self-help, the Pygmalion effect can be a powerful tool for personal growth and development.

For example, a teacher who believes that one of her students is very smart and will do very well academically. That teacher will definitely give more attention, encouragement and help to the child. She is putting this extra effort not just because of the love for that student. It is very important for the teacher that her belief and prediction are correct. Similarly, this student will also try not to break the faith and hope of the teacher. Thus, favorable circumstances, encouragement, and determination help the student to live up to the expectations of his beloved teacher.

When we believe something about ourselves, we are more likely to act in ways that are consistent with our beliefs. Thus, we reinforce those beliefs of ours and encourage the same behavior. Similarly, when we believe something about others, we may act in ways that encourage them to confirm our assumptions. Thus, our beliefs about them will be strengthened. We don't think much about these cycles when the results are positive, but when the results are negative there is a common term for these cycles - Vicious Cycles.

Here are some ways in which the Pygmalion effect can manifest in self-help:

1. **Self-fulfilling prophecies:** When a person has a strong belief or expectation about their ability to achieve a certain goal, they are more likely to take the necessary steps to make it happen. For example, if someone believes they can lose weight and get fit, they are more likely to exercise regularly and eat a healthy diet.
2. **Confidence and motivation:** When a person believes in their own abilities, they are more likely to feel confident and motivated to take action. This can lead to a positive feedback loop, where success breeds further confidence and motivation.
3. **Overcoming limiting beliefs:** The Pygmalion effect can also help people overcome limiting beliefs and negative self-talk that may be holding them back. By adopting a growth mindset and believing in their ability to change, people can overcome obstacles and achieve their goals.
4. **Placebo effect:** The Pygmalion effect can also be influenced by the placebo effect, where a person's belief in a particular outcome can actually produce the desired result. For example, if someone believes that a certain self-help technique will work for them, they are more likely to experience positive results.
5. **Social influence:** The Pygmalion effect can also be influenced by social norms and expectations. When a person is surrounded by others who believe in their ability to achieve a certain goal, they are more likely to adopt that belief themselves. This can be seen in the power of social support networks and accountability partners in self-help.

16. Single Cause Fallacy

Everything in life is often much more complex than it seems. For example, questions like why a problem arose, why a political party faced defeat there, or why a company incurred losses, all have numerous factors and components contributing to them. However, human minds tend to seek a single cause to grasp and understand the complexity. The single cause fallacy is a cognitive bias where a person attributes a single cause to a complex issue or problem. This fallacy is common in self-help literature and media, where a single solution or strategy is often presented as the answer to a person's problems.

Examples of the single cause fallacy in self-help include:

1. **"The secret to success is...":** Self-help books and seminars often promote a single formula or strategy as the key to success. However, success is a complex and multifaceted concept that cannot be reduced to a single cause.
2. **"The one thing you need to do to lose weight is...":** Weight loss is a complex issue that involves many factors, including diet, exercise, genetics, and lifestyle. However, some self-help resources might suggest that a single factor, such as a specific diet or exercise routine, is the key to weight loss.
3. **"The reason you're unhappy is because...":** Self-help resources might suggest that a single factor, such as a person's mindset or a specific life event, is the cause of their unhappiness. However, happiness is a complex emotion that can be influenced by many factors.

Though severe problems might have straightforward solutions and easily applicable remedies, human beings frequently resort to attributing such problems to a single cause for simplicity. This is where the Single Cause Fallacy comes into play. It involves oversimplifying intricate problems and suggesting that they can be solved by addressing just one aspect.

For instance, many people readily advise that the main reason for your failure might be your lack of self-confidence. This notion is often propagated by self-help books and motivational figures who tend to follow common patterns. In reality, your success isn't solely tied to a single factor like your intelligence, work style, or luck. Countless unseen variables could contribute to either your success or failure.

The self-help industry often promotes the idea that you can transform your life overnight by changing your mindset. Unfortunately, they often overlook external factors, shifts in our thinking, distortions, and influencing elements. It's important to note that while single cause fallacy can be harmful, it's not always intentional. Sometimes, self-help resources might oversimplify complex issues unintentionally or due to limited understanding.

The Gamblers world

The gambler's fallacy is a cognitive bias that can be present in various industries, including the self-help industry. The gambler's fallacy refers to the mistaken belief that a random event, such as the toss of a coin, is more likely to happen if it hasn't happened recently, or less likely to happen if it has happened recently.

Imagine a life where failures happen repeatedly, whether in personal matters, business, or other areas. Observers often hold the person or their actions responsible for these recurring failures. Similarly, when numerous individuals criticize someone facing frequent failure or numerous misfortunes, it's convenient to assume that the underlying cause might be their own mistakes.

In the context of the self-help industry, the gambler's fallacy can manifest in a few ways:

1. **Success stories:** Self-help books, seminars, and online courses often feature success stories of individuals who have achieved their goals through the program or technique being promoted. However, these success stories may create an unrealistic expectation that the program will work for everyone, ignoring the fact that success is often the result of a combination of factors, including hard work, luck, and privilege.
2. **Testimonials:** Testimonials from satisfied customers can be a powerful marketing tool for self-help products and services. However, testimonials can also be misleading if they create the impression that the product or service is responsible for the customer's success, when in reality, other factors may have played a more significant role.
3. **Guarantees:** Some self-help products and services offer guarantees or promises of success. For example, a course may promise that participants will earn a certain amount of money or achieve a specific goal within a certain timeframe. However,

these guarantees are often based on an unrealistic assumption that the program is the sole determinant of success, ignoring the role of external factors. Some self-help programs may create the impression that positive thinking is enough to overcome any obstacle, which is not supported by scientific evidence.

According to the just-world hypothesis, people tend to attribute misfortunes to someone's actions because they believe in a just world where fairness prevails in the end. However, this isn't always the case. It's crucial to remember that what the majority believes isn't always true. For instance, at one time, the entire world believed the Earth was flat, and everyone believed the sun orbited around the Earth. Initially, only one or two individuals held a different perspective, which eventually turned out to be correct. The general population isn't always accurate.

The World of Dice

Now, let's consider the probability of failure occurring in succession. Here, we encounter the cognitive bias known as the 'Gambler's Fallacy' and the injustice in the 'Just World' theory. When you flip a coin, the chance of it landing on heads or tails is 50%. This means that if it lands on heads once, it doesn't guarantee it will be tails the next time. Similarly, if you flip a coin 10 times and get heads 9 times, it doesn't mean that tails will come up next. According to mathematics, if you flip a coin five times and get heads each time, the odds of getting heads again or tails are the same. Similarly, if you flip a coin ten times and get heads every time, the likelihood of getting heads or tails remains consistent. Therefore, attributing failures solely to bad luck, without considering prior circumstances, lacks justification and can lead to misunderstanding.

In summary, it's essential to recognize that failures can occur due to various factors, including external circumstances beyond one's control. It's unfair to assume that someone's actions are the sole cause of their failures, especially when we don't have all the information. Instead, we should strive for a more nuanced understanding of the situation and avoid jumping to conclusions based on cognitive biases.

7. Common Self-Help Myths

Psychology, as a scientific discipline, explores the complexities of human behavior and mental processes. This multifaceted field draws insights from various areas such as neurology, genetics, evolution, and anthropology. However, there is a common misconception that psychology aligns with mere common sense. This misunderstanding often leads individuals to believe they understand psychology based on personal experiences or intuition. Unfortunately, these interpretations are often inaccurate and misleading.

These popular interpretations of psychology, based on personal imagination, experiences, and whims, lack any scientific foundation. The theories propagated by motivational figures are better termed as "backyard psychology." In popular culture, this type of "armchair psychology" often prevails.

Armchair psychology is not only inaccurate but also potentially harmful. It can lead individuals to make unwise life choices, impacting both their own lives and those of others whom they influence. Moreover, it can perpetuate stereotypes and misunderstandings regarding mental health.

Unfortunately, pop psychologists have spread numerous myths about brain function and human behavior. Regrettably, these misconceptions have sometimes been mistaken as established scientific truths. Let us now examine some widely embraced myths fostered by popular psychology.

1. Smile is the secret of happiness

Positive psychology has gained significant popularity in recent times. According to its proponents, a simple smile can instantly make you happy, even on a bad day. It sounds wonderful, doesn't it? Who wouldn't want to experience happiness so easily? It's essential to recognize that a smile alone cannot solve all our problems or erase the unhappiness caused by negative events. Furthermore, the notion that we should be happy all the time is unrealistic and can even be detrimental to our well-being. Putting on a fake smile won't truly heal someone who is grieving or facing profound.

However, one of the main weaknesses of positive psychology is its excessive focus on positive emotions and experiences, while neglecting the importance of negative emotions and experiences. This approach leads to a superficial and incomplete understanding of human psychology, overlooking the significant role that negative emotions play in shaping our lives.

Moreover, positive psychology tends to prioritize personal happiness and well-being, while neglecting the broader social and cultural factors that influence mental health. This approach pushes for a quick fix without delving into the underlying psychological or social factors that contribute to mental health problems.

It is important to acknowledge and address our emotions genuinely and authentically. Positive psychology has its merits, no doubt, but it's essential to adopt a more scientific approach that considers the complexity of human emotions and experiences. By acknowledging and addressing both positive and negative emotions, we can work towards a more comprehensive understanding of mental health and well-being.

2. Power Posing

Power posing, a theory popularized by social psychologist Amy Cuddy's 2010 TED talk, suggests that assuming a strong, expansive posture can boost confidence, reduce stress, and enhance performance in high-pressure situations.

This theory is based on the notion that body language can influence our emotional states and physiological processes. According to this idea, adopting a posture of confidence and strength, often referred to as the "Wonder Woman" pose, leads to increased testosterone levels and reduced cortisol, the stress hormone.

However, research has shown that the effectiveness of power posing is likely a myth. In 2010, a study published in the journal Psychological Science found that participants who adopted high-power poses (e.g., expansive, open body language) did not experience an increase in feelings of power or confidence, compared to those who adopted low-power poses (e.g., closed, restrictive body language).

Furthermore, a 2018 review of 55 studies on power posing found that the evidence for its effectiveness was weak and inconsistent. The review concluded that power posing has little to no impact on cognitive, emotional, or behavioral outcomes.

There are several reasons why power posing may not be effective:

While adopting expansive body language may make people feel more confident in some situations, it is not a reliable way to boost confidence or power. People's emotions and behaviors are influenced by a wide range of factors, including their thoughts, beliefs, and context.

When people adopt expansive body language in situations where it is not naturally occurring, it may come across as forced or artificial. This can undermine the intended effect and potentially make people feel uncomfortable or suspicious.

The effectiveness of power posing may vary across cultures and individuals. Some people may find expansive body language to be assertive or dominant, while others may see it as aggressive or confrontational.

If people believe that adopting certain body language will make them feel more confident, they may experience a placebo effect, where their confidence increases regardless of the actual body language they adopt.

3. Opposites attract

The concept of "opposites attract" is a common belief that people with opposite personalities, values, or interests are attracted to each other and are more likely to form a romantic relationship. However, research has shown that this belief is largely a myth.

There are several reasons why the concept of opposites attracting may be a myth. One reason is that people tend to be attracted to those who are similar to themselves, as mentioned earlier. Another reason is that people may be more likely to notice and remember instances where opposites do attract, which can create a biased perception of the relationship landscape. Additionally, the idea of opposites attracting may be a cultural trope that is perpetuated in media and popular culture, which can also contribute to the perception that it is a common phenomenon.

We could sometime spot cases where people with opposite interest getting attracted. But the scientific consensus is that the concept of opposites attracting is largely a myth. People tend to be attracted to those who are similar to themselves in terms of personality, values, and interests, and this similarity is a key factor in determining the success and satisfaction of a relationship.

4. Group decisions are always superior

The notion that group decisions are always superior is a misconception. In reality, many times group decisions turn out to be disastrous. This is due to various psychological factors that impact the effectiveness of group collaboration. Let us have a closer look at this phenomenon.

Groupthink: The Silent Killer of Sound Decision-Making

Groupthink describes the phenomenon where a group of individuals, who are collectively intelligent and well-intentioned, make irrational or poor decisions. This occurs when the group's desire for unanimity and the avoidance of conflict overshadows their ability to critically evaluate ideas and consider alternative perspectives. The result is a decision that is not only flawed but also potentially disastrous.

The Bay of Pigs invasion of Cuba is a prime example of groupthink. President Kennedy and his team, consisting of seasoned diplomats and military officers, were convinced that a small force of 1,400 soldiers would be sufficient to overthrow the Cuban government. They were blinded by their own confidence and failed to consider the obvious risks involved. The invasion ended in catastrophe, with the majority of the troops being killed or captured.

Another example of groupthink is the attack on Pearl Harbor. US officials were aware of Japan's preparations for an attack, but they dismissed the threat, believing that Japan would never dare attack Hawaii. They were convinced that the US would emerge victorious in any potential conflict, and thus, they failed to take adequate measures to prepare for a possible attack. The result was a surprise attack that left over 2,400 people dead and a significant blow to the US naval fleet.

Groupthink can be attributed to a number of factors, including:

When a group lacks diversity in terms of background, experience, and perspectives, they are more likely to fall victim to groupthink. Without differing viewpoints, there is no challenge to the dominant idea, and the group tends to accept it without question.

When a group is highly cohesive, members are reluctant to disagree with one another, fearing that it may disrupt the group's unity. This leads to a lack of open discussion and critical evaluation of ideas.

A dominant leader can exert pressure on the group to conform to their ideas, discouraging dissent and alternative perspectives.

Group members may share similar beliefs, values, and experiences, leading to a narrow and biased view of the situation. When a group lacks access to relevant information or chooses to ignore it, they are more likely to make poor decisions.

The consequences of groupthink can be severe, as seen in the examples of the Bay of Pigs invasion and the attack on Pearl Harbor. In both cases, the failure to critically evaluate ideas and consider alternative perspectives led to devastating outcomes.

5. Venting Out Your Emotions - Catharsis

Venting out your emotions, also known as catharsis, is a common belief that releasing pent-up emotions can help to reduce stress and anxiety. However, research has shown that this approach may not be effective in the long run and can potentially do more harm than good. Here are some reasons why venting out your emotions may not be a good thing:

When you vent out your emotions, you may feel a temporary release of tension, but it can also reinforce the negative emotions you're feeling. This can make it harder to move on from the emotions and can keep you stuck in a cycle of negativity.

Venting out your emotions can be counterproductive because it can make you feel worse in the long run. Studies have shown that people who engage in catharsis tend to feel more angry, sad, and anxious afterwards.

Here you may end up saying things that you shouldn't have said, which can damage relationships with friends, family, and colleagues. Venting out your emotions can make you feel vulnerable and exposed, which can be uncomfortable and even embarrassing.

It's not a long-term solution: Venting out your emotions may provide temporary relief, but it's not a long-term solution to managing stress and anxiety. It's important to address the root causes of your emotions and develop healthier coping mechanisms.

So, what can you do instead of venting out your emotions? Here are some alternative strategies:

Mindfulness is a powerful tool for managing emotions. It involves being present in the moment, observing your emotions without judgment, and taking deep breaths.

Engage in physical activity: Exercise is a great way to release tension and improve your mood. It can help to reduce stress and anxiety by releasing endorphins, which are natural mood-boosters.

Writing in a journal can help you process your emotions and gain perspective. It's a healthy way to express your feelings without venting them out to others.

If you need to talk to someone, choose a trusted friend or therapist who can provide support and guidance. They can help you develop healthier coping strategies and work through your emotions in a productive way.

Focusing on what you're grateful for can help shift your perspective and improve your mood. It's a healthy way to redirect your emotions and cultivate a positive mindset.

Remember, managing emotions is a process that takes time and effort. It's important to develop healthy coping mechanisms that work for you in the long run, rather than relying on venting out your emotions as a quick fix.

6. You are either left/right brained

The concept that people are either left-brained or right-brained, meaning that they are more logical and analytical or more creative and intuitive, respectively, is a popular myth. This idea has been debunked by scientists and experts in the field of neuroscience and psychology. Let us look at the ground reality of this aspect.

Contrary to popular belief, the human brain is not divided into two distinct hemispheres, one for logic and analysis and the other for creativity and intuition. In reality, both hemispheres are involved in most cognitive tasks, and they work together in a coordinated manner.

There is no clear definition of what constitutes a "left-brained" or "right-brained" person. The terms were originally coined by psychologist Roger Sperry in the 1960s to describe the different ways in which the brain processes information, but they have since been misinterpreted and oversimplified.

There is no scientific evidence to support the idea that people can be categorized into two distinct groups based on their brain hemisphere dominance. Studies have shown that both hemispheres are involved in a wide range of cognitive tasks, and that individuals are not strictly left- or right-brained.

The human brain is a complex and dynamic organ, and its function cannot be reduced to a simple left-brained/right-brained dichotomy. Different brain regions work together in a coordinated manner to perform various cognitive tasks, and individuals are not limited to one specific mode of thinking.

The idea of left-brained and right-brained thinking has been influenced by cultural and societal factors, such as the emphasis on logic and reason in Western culture. This has led to a bias towards viewing certain cognitive abilities as "left-brained" and others as "right-brained."

The left-brained/right-brained dichotomy has not been found to be a useful predictor of success or performance in various fields, such as art, science, mathematics, or engineering.

In reality, the concept of left-brained and right-brained thinking is a myth that has been perpetuated by popular culture and misinterpretation of scientific research. The human brain is a complex and dynamic organ that cannot be reduced to a simple dichotomy, and individuals are not limited to one specific mode of thinking.

7. Are men and women from two planets?

People have been arguing for a long time about whether men and women are completely different. Even Dr. Sigmund Freud, the father of modern psychology, once brought up this question with his student Maria Bonaparte, who was the grandniece of Napoleon Bonaparte. He said, "What do women really want?" I've been thinking about this for a very long thirty years! Surprisingly, I still don't have a clear answer.

Many psychologists, scientists, and even TV and movies suggest that men and women are fundamentally different. Men are often depicted discussing topics such as sports, food, books, politics, and other intellectual pursuits. In contrast, women are frequently shown talking about feelings, friendships, clothes, kids, and cooking. Additionally, many people believe that women are better at understanding emotions and being kind.

Some motivational speakers even claim that men and women are like completely different species.

Example

"Mars and Venus Series" - John Gray

John Gray, an American "folk psychologist," gained fame by proposing that men and women come from separate planets. His best-selling "Mars and Venus" series of books has sold over 50 million copies in forty-three languages. When it comes to his academic credentials-Gray holds a degree in meditation and a post-graduate diploma in psychology. Remarkably, his "Mars and Venus" series ranks among the 25 most influential books of the 20th century.

Gray contends that the dissimilarities between men and women extend far beyond communication; their thoughts, emotions, reactions, affections, and desires are fundamentally different. He perceives them as distinct creatures from two distant planets. Women tend to openly express their emotions when upset, whereas men retreat into their own solitary burrows.

Now, let's delve into his primary arguments concerning gender differences:

Gray argues that men and women have different communication styles. Men tend to use a more direct and assertive style, while women use a more indirect and emotional style. He suggests that women are more comfortable expressing their emotions than men. Women tend to openly express their emotions when upset, whereas men retreat into their own solitary burrows.

Gray proposes that men and women react differently to stress. Men tend to become more aggressive and competitive when stressed, while women tend to become more emotional and nurturing. According to his theory t men and women have different desires and affections. Men tend to desire power and control, while women desire intimacy and connection.

a. Women talk more than men

The idea that women talk significantly more than men was originally presented by psychiatrist Louann Brizendine in her book "The Female Brain." In her book, she asserts that women speak 20,000 words a day compared to men's 200 words. Unfortunately, this misinformation was later widely embraced as a scientific truth. However, it was later revealed that this information was founded on speculations from a self-help book and lacked substantial evidence. This is just another misconception that has been perpetuated by popular media and self-help books.

b. Women are more likely to reveal their personal details than men

There is a common notion that women are more likely to share personal details than men. However, this notion lacks a universal basis and is not always accurate. In reality, the willingness to share personal information varies among individuals and can depend on various factors, such as personality, upbringing, and cultural background. In some cases, men might be more open in revealing personal information than women.

c. Men are more likely to interrupt

The notion that men are generally more likely to interrupt others while talking is not an absolute rule. It depends on various factors such as an individual's personality, social status, cultural background, and communication style. In different societies, both men and women may exhibit higher or lower tendencies to interrupt.

It's important to note that interruptions can occur in any gender, and it's not a fixed trait. People's communication styles and behaviors can change based on various factors, and it's not accurate to make generalizations about a group of people based on their gender.

d. Do women have a better ability than men to read non-verbal cues from body language?

The belief that women possess a superior ability to interpret non-verbal cues through body language compared to men is widely accepted. However, the differences in this aspect are minor and can be influenced by cultural norms, individual variations, and the environment in which people live.

In other words, the idea that women are naturally better at reading non-verbal cues is a stereotype that is not supported by scientific evidence. While there may be some differences in how men and women interpret body language, these differences are relatively small and can be influenced by a variety of factors.

8. Problems of middle age

In many societies, there is a prevailing belief that middle age in a person's life is a time of complex problems. The period between forty-five and sixty is often considered a time of significant challenges. During this phase, people encounter various issues such as confusion, forgetfulness, changes in sexual desires, parenting difficulties with growing children, work-related stress, and the loss of parents, among other things.

While early pioneers of psychology like Sigmund Freud, Carl Jung, and Erik Erikson did discuss the complexities of middle age, like many other theories of these pioneers, this middle age crisis was not grounded in or backed by experimental evidence. The idea that middle age is a time of crisis or decline is a myth that has been perpetuated by societal expectations and stereotypes. Here are some reasons why this myth is not supported by scientific evidence:

While some people may experience a midlife crisis, it is not a universal experience that affects everyone in middle age. In fact, research suggests that the majority of people do not experience a midlife crisis.

Contrary to the stereotype that middle age is a time of crisis, research suggests that it is actually a time of stability and emotional maturity. Many people in middle age have established their careers, built strong relationships, and have a sense of fulfilment and purpose.

Studies have shown that happiness is not determined by age. People of all ages can experience happiness and fulfilment, and middle age is no exception. It can be a time of personal growth and renewal, as people reflect on their lives and consider new opportunities and experiences. This can lead to a sense of revitalization and renewed purpose.

Stereotype of middle age as a time of crisis can be harmful, as it can create unnecessary anxiety and pressure for people in this age group. It can also lead to ageism, which can limit opportunities for older adults.

9. Personality becomes stable as you mature

The idea that personality becomes stable as you mature is a myth because personality is not fixed and can continue to evolve and change throughout a person's life. Here are some reasons why this myth is not supported by scientific evidence:

Personality is shaped by a combination of genetic, environmental, and cultural factors, and these influences can change over time. For example, a person's environment, social relationships, and life experiences can all impact their personality. Research has shown that personality can change over time, and that people can experience significant changes in their personality traits as they age. For example, some studies have found that older adults tend to be more conscientious and agreeable than younger adults.

The brain continues to develop and change throughout a person's life, and this can impact personality. For example, research has shown that the prefrontal cortex, which is responsible for decision-making and other executive functions, continues to develop and mature well into adulthood.

Major life events, such as marriage, parenthood, or a career change, can impact a person's personality. For example, a person who experiences a major stressful event may become more anxious or depressed. Personality is not a fixed trait, and it can change in response to a variety of factors. For example, a person who is typically extroverted may become more introverted after a stressful experience.

Cultural and societal factors can also impact personality. For example, a person who grows up in a collectivist culture may be more likely to be agreeable and cooperative, while a person who grows up in an individualist culture may be more likely to be independent and self-assertive. Personality is a complex and dynamic trait that can continue to evolve and change throughout a person's life, and it is influenced by a variety of factors, including genetics, environment, and life experiences.

10. Dreams are royal roads to the unconscious

Dreams are often considered the royal roads to the unconscious. This belief has been deeply ingrained in cultures worldwide, with ancient civilizations like Rome, Greece, Egypt, and India interpreting dreams as messengers of the gods. Despite the passage of time and advances in modern medicine, many societies continue to believe that dreams hold predictive meanings. In countries like America, Korea, and India, a study revealed that a significant portion of people, ranging from 56% to 74%, still cling to the notion that dreams carry mysterious messages.

Sigmund Freud, the father of modern psychology, believed dreams to be veiled expressions of our suppressed desires. His influential book "The Interpretation of Dreams" delved into this concept, shaping dream analysis as a vital aspect of Freudian psychotherapy. However, subsequent advancements in medicine and psychology have strongly challenged Freud's theory of dreams.

What Modern Medicine Has to Say About Dreams

The Neurobiological Theory

This theory proposes that dreams are a result of the brain's neural activity during sleep, and are influenced by various neurotransmitters and brain regions. This theory suggests that dreams can provide insight into the workings of the brain and can help us to understand various neurological and psychiatric disorders.

The Activation-Synthesis Model

Modern medicine puts forth the activation-synthesis theory as one of the prominent perspectives on dreams. This theory, developed by psychologists Dr. John Allen Hobson and Dr. Robert McCarley from Harvard University, proposes that dreams are a result of the brain's attempt to make sense of random neural activity that occurs during sleep. According to this model, the brain takes fragments of memories, thoughts, and other stimuli from the day and synthesizes them into a coherent narrative, resulting in a dream. To put it simply, even during sleep, the lower parts of our brain remain highly active, controlling fundamental bodily functions like heart rate, while other brain regions handle analysis and perception. Dreams occur when these regions interpret the activities of the aforementioned brain parts.

The Content of Dreams

Regarding the content of dreams, certain emotions are consistently expressed. Happiness emerges as the most prevalent emotion in dreams, followed by anxiety, fear, and anger. All the emotions and visions experienced in dreams are reflections of our daytime experiences and feelings.

Dreams can be influenced by hidden anxieties and our physical and mental conditions. However, the scenes and feelings in dreams are often illogical and disconnected. Dreams consist of a random collection of experiences and emotions, lacking a coherent order. Hence, ascribing profound meanings to most dreams would be misguided since they usually hold no significant purpose.

11. The 10% Brain

You may have heard the idea that even the brilliant Albert Einstein only used 10% of his brain. This notion, while motivating, is far from true and has become a favorite theme of motivational speakers. They often talk about unlocking the untapped power of the human brain, asserting that 90% of it remains untapped. However, let's explore the origins of this 10% concept.

About a century ago, renowned psychologist William James once mentioned, "I doubt whether we are making use of our possible mental and physical resources." This notion evolved over time into the belief that we only use 10% of our brain's capacity, exciting and inspiring listeners. This notion persists in popular culture, despite efforts to dispel it (Hughes, Lyddy, & Lamb, 2013). The movie Lucy (2014) was based on this idea, imagining the potential of using all 100% of one's brainpower. Pseudoscientific psychic abilities and self-help programs also use it to justify their claims of unlocking hidden human potential. Hughes et al. (2013) found that this misconception (referred to as the 10% Myth) is widespread. Even more concerning, Dekker et al. (2012) discovered that around 50% of primary and secondary teachers from various cultures also endorse this myth.

The idea that humans only use 10% of their brains is a common myth that has been debunked by experts in neuroscience and psychology. Here are some reasons why this myth is not supported by scientific evidence:

Modern brain imaging techniques such as functional magnetic resonance imaging (fMRI), positron emission tomography (PET), and electroencephalography (EEG) have shown that almost all areas of the brain are active during various cognitive tasks and mental processes. This contradicts the idea that only a small percentage of the brain is used.

The brain has the ability to reorganize and adapt throughout life, a process known as neuroplasticity. This means that different areas of the brain can take over functions that are normally performed by other areas, making it unlikely that only 10% of the brain is used.

Studies of people who have suffered brain damage have shown that even small lesions in certain areas of the brain can have significant effects on cognition and behavior. This suggests that different areas of the brain are specialized for specific functions and are not redundant, as would be expected if only 10% of the brain were used.

The brain is a highly energy-demanding organ, and it is unlikely that evolution would have favored the development of a brain that is largely unused. The brain is thought to have evolved to optimize cognitive abilities and to be efficient in terms of energy usage.

Many cognitive processes, such as language, memory, attention, and problem-solving, involve the coordination of multiple areas of the brain. This suggests that the brain is highly interconnected and that different areas work together to perform complex tasks, rather than only a small percentage of the brain being used.

While it is true that some areas of the brain are more active at certain times than others, and that some people may use certain areas of their brains more than others, it is not accurate to say that only a small percentage of the brain is used.

Other Common Misconceptions

1. Misconception: Maternal mental stress during pregnancy causes miscarriage.

Explanation: There is no scientific evidence supporting the notion that maternal mental stress causes miscarriage.

2. Myth: The psychological bond between mother and baby forms in just a few minutes after birth.

Explanation: The emotional connection between a mother and her baby develops gradually and is influenced by various factors beyond the initial moments after birth.

3. Myth: Children need parental encouragement to learn how to walk.

Explanation: Children's ability to walk and achieve developmental milestones is primarily determined by their physical readiness, not solely reliant on external encouragement.

4. Myth: Children do not lie or keep secrets.

Explanation: At a young age, children may hide their thoughts and feelings, and they can also demonstrate skill in telling lies.

5. Myth: Adopted children are prone to compromised mental health.

Explanation: Adoption does not automatically lead to mental health issues in children; it is not a direct cause of mental health problems.

6. Myth: The presence of children increases psychological harmony and satisfaction between couples.

Explanation: In reality, after the birth of the first child, marital satisfaction and unity may decrease, but over time, they can gradually regain that unity.

7. Myth: Older people are more afraid of death.

Explanation: Older individuals tend to fear death less as they come to accept its inevitability. Additionally, with fewer obligations and desires, they may experience less fear compared to younger individuals.

8. Myth: Some terminally ill people postpone their death until a certain day.

Explanation: While this idea lacks absolute truth, there is limited evidence suggesting that some women with cancer may pass away close to their birthdays.

9. Myth: The majority of domestic violence is perpetrated by men.

Explanation: Both men and women commit acts of domestic violence in equal numbers.

10. Myth: Smoking cessation requires de-addiction treatment, parallel treatment, and religious interventions.

Explanation: Many people are able to quit smoking on their own without any external help.

11. Myth: The "Mozart Effect" - The popular notion that listening to classical music, particularly Mozart's, can enhance intelligence has been widely promoted. However, there is no concrete evidence supporting this claim. While music can positively affect mood and cognition, research hasn't proven its significant impact on IQ or academic performance.

12. Myth: People are either introverts or extroverts - In reality, a person's personality is multifaceted and cannot be simply categorized. While some individuals may lean towards introversion or extroversion, most fall somewhere in the middle of this spectrum.

13. Myth: The intelligence of every individual is fixed and cannot be changed - Although genetics do play a role in intelligence, research has conclusively shown that the brain possesses the ability to change and grow. Intelligence can be enhanced through effort and practice.

14. Myth: Hypnosis is a magical state in which people lose self-control - While people may become more compliant during hypnotic states, they remain fully aware and in control of their actions.

15. Myth: All mental health problems are caused by childhood experiences - While early experiences impact mental health, contemporary science shows that genetics, brain chemistry, life events, and social factors also contribute to mental health problems.

16. Myth: Self-esteem is the key to happiness - While healthy self-esteem is vital, solely focusing on building it can be counterproductive. Research suggests that self-compassion is a more effective path to happiness.

17. Myth: Positive emotions are always good, negative emotions are always bad - While fostering positive emotions is beneficial, negative emotions can also serve a purpose. The key is finding a balance between the two in life.

18. Myth: Effects of Subliminal Messages: Subliminal messages have subtle effects on human behavior, but popular psychology tends to exaggerate their effectiveness. Research shows that the impact of subliminal messages is limited and context-dependent.

19. Myth: Depression is simply the result of negative thinking - Negative thoughts can contribute to depression, but it is a complex mental health disorder influenced by genetics, brain chemistry, life events, and social factors.

20. Myth: Mindfulness means always being calm - While mindfulness can promote relaxation, its goal is not to eliminate all negative emotions or achieve a constant state of bliss.

21. Myth: Memory works like a video recorder - Our beliefs about memory often don't align with reality. Memory is not like a flawless digital recorder that captures, stores, and retrieves information perfectly. It comprises a collection of scattered images, information, and feelings, which may be rewritten over time due to various factors.

22. Myth: Nostalgia is always positive - Nostalgia can evoke warm and comforting feelings, but it can also carry sadness and longing.

23. Myth: Being in love means never having quarrels - While love fosters connection and togetherness, conflicts and disagreements are normal in intimate relationships and can actually strengthen the partnership.

24. Myth: Achieving More Through Multitasking: Though multitasking may appear to increase productivity by handling multiple tasks simultaneously, research reveals that it actually decreases efficiency and leads to more errors. Shifting brain energy from one task to another can be counterproductive.

25. Myth: Happiness as Life's Ultimate Goal: While happiness is a desirable emotion, considering it the sole ultimate goal in life may not yield the desired results. Studies show that focusing on the meaning and purpose behind our actions leads to better psychological well-being.

26. Myth: Positive Thinking and Physical Healing: A positive outlook can have positive effects on overall health, but it should not be seen as a substitute for medical treatment. Scientific evidence does not support the notion that positive thinking can heal physical ailments.

27. Myth: Financial gain is the ultimate gain: Financial stability is crucial for success, but true success is not solely measured by high income and material wealth. Personal fulfillment, meaningful relationships, and making a positive impact on society are essential factors in determining success in life.

8. Believe In Your Own Abilities: A Double-Edged Sword

The power of self-belief is often touted as the key to achieving anything in life. We're frequently told, "Believe in your own abilities, and you can conquer the world." It's an inspiring message, and there's no denying that self-reliance and confidence are valuable qualities that can lead to personal growth and accomplishments. However, is blind faith in our own abilities always a good thing? Is there a downside to excessive confidence?

Let's delve into an example to explore this further:

Imagine a person who has been showered with praise since childhood. As they grow older, their confidence skyrockets, and they start believing they can handle any task or challenge without seeking assistance. They become convinced that they know best in every situation and reject the help and advice of others, even when faced with potential danger.

However, individuals with such unwavering confidence may experience several drawbacks:

Unrealistic Expectations

One of the main problems with too much positive thinking is that it can create unrealistic expectations. When we constantly focus on the positive aspects of life, we can start to believe that everything will always go our way and that we will never encounter any obstacles. This can lead to a sense of entitlement and a lack of preparedness for the challenges that life inevitably throws our way.

Lack of Resilience

When we are constantly shielded from negative thoughts and emotions, we can become ill-equipped to handle difficult situations. Resilience is built by facing challenges and learning to overcome them, but if we are too focused on the positive, we may not develop the skills we need to bounce back from adversity.

Denial of Reality

Another problem with too much positive thinking is that it can lead to denial of reality. When we focus solely on the positive, we may start to ignore the negative aspects of our lives. This can lead to a lack of awareness of potential problems and a failure to address them. By denying the existence of problems, we may actually make them worse.

Disconnection from Emotions

Positive thinking can also lead to a disconnection from our emotions. When we constantly focus on the positive, we may start to suppress our negative emotions. This can lead to a lack of emotional intelligence and an inability to understand and process our emotions in a healthy way.

Lack of Empathy

Too much positive thinking can also lead to a lack of empathy. When we are overly focused on the positive, we may start to view others who are struggling as weak or negative. This can lead to a lack of understanding and support for those who are going through difficult times.

Overemphasis on Individualism

Positive thinking can also lead to an overemphasis on individualism. When we focus solely on our own positive thoughts and emotions, we may start to neglect the importance of community and social connections. This can lead to feelings of isolation and loneliness.

Neglect of Systemic Issues

Finally, too much positive thinking can lead to a neglect of systemic issues. When we focus solely on the positive, we may start to ignore the larger social and economic problems that affect our communities. By neglecting these issues, we may fail to address the root causes of poverty, inequality, and other social ills.

Neglecting Others' Perspectives

By dismissing others' perspectives, they may overlook valuable insights, constructive criticism, or alternative approaches that could lead to better outcomes. By believing they know it all and don't need others, they fail to learn from the experiences of those around them. They become unable to acknowledge their own weaknesses, which restricts their potential for personal and professional development.

Constantly rejecting the opinions of others can make it difficult for them to connect with people, leading to isolation in both personal and professional spheres. Overconfidence can hinder their ability to thoroughly analyze problems, leading to hasty and ill-informed decisions with negative consequences.

Isolation and Hasty Decisions

They strive to handle everything on their own, constantly trying to prove their abilities. This self-imposed burden can result in immense physical, mental, financial, and social stress. By refusing to cooperate or seek help from others, they may miss out on opportunities for integration and innovative problem-solving.

The Burden of Self-Reliance

The constant need to maintain their self-image can take a toll on their mental well-being if they feel unable to live up to their own expectations.

The Toll on Mental Well-being

It's important to remember that self-belief should not hinder us from seeking support from others. Acknowledging our weaknesses and being open to making changes is crucial for success in both personal and professional aspects of life. Mutual cooperation and humility play vital roles in achieving our goals.

It's also worth noting that success can be achieved by individuals who initially lack self-confidence. In fact, people with low self-esteem often possess an underlying insecurity that motivates them to work harder and reach their goals. Interestingly, this insecurity can serve as a source of motivation on occasion.

While belief in our abilities is a positive trait, blind confidence can have negative consequences. Striking a balance between self-assurance and humility is essential. Recognizing the value of seeking help and advice from others allows us to achieve success while maintaining healthy relationships and avoiding the adverse effects of excessive confidence.

When Positivity Turns Toxic

Toxic positivity can be detrimental to our mental health and overall well-being. It dismisses genuine emotions and pressures individuals to mask their struggles, denying them the opportunity to process and heal. It often manifests in statements such as "just be happy," "good vibes only," or "everything happens for a reason." While these phrases may be well-intentioned, they can invalidate the complexities of human emotions.

The Dangers of Toxic Positivity:

a. Emotional Suppression: Encouraging only positive emotions can lead individuals to suppress or ignore their genuine feelings. This can create a cycle of emotional avoidance, preventing healthy emotional processing and potentially leading to long-term negative consequences.

b. Invalidating Experiences: Toxic positivity dismisses the validity of negative experiences, making individuals feel guilty or ashamed for experiencing natural emotions such as sadness, anger, or grief. This invalidation can lead to feelings of isolation and further emotional distress.

c. Pressure to Always Be Positive: The pressure to maintain a positive facade can be exhausting and unrealistic. It creates an environment where individuals feel compelled to hide their struggles, leading to feelings of inadequacy and a lack of authentic connection with others.

Embracing Authenticity and Emotional Well-being

Honouring All Emotions: Instead of suppressing or denying negative emotions, it is important to acknowledge and validate them. Allowing ourselves to feel and process a full range of emotions fosters emotional growth and resilience.

Treat yourself with kindness and understanding, recognizing that it is natural to experience a mix of positive and negative emotions. Offer yourself the same compassion you would extend to a friend facing challenges.

Surround yourself with individuals who allow you to express your authentic emotions without judgment. Seek out genuine connections where you can share both triumphs and struggles, fostering a sense of understanding and empathy.

Instead of forcing positivity, focus on cultivating a positive mindset through mindfulness and gratitude. Mindful positivity acknowledges the challenges while seeking opportunities for growth and finding gratitude in the present moment.

An Anecdote of Misguided Medical Optimism

Recently a family friend of mine contacted me about a heartbreaking situation. Her husband, a strong man in his mid-70s, had been fighting cancer for five long years. At first, the treatments seemed hopeful, but unfortunately, the cancer spread throughout his body. For the past year, he had been receiving palliative care since there was no specific treatment available.

Sadly, his health took a turn for the worse in the past few months. He experienced intense pain, hallucinations, and thoughts of death. His wife was concerned about their new doctor, who stopped his medication due to worries about side effects. Instead, the doctor suggested finding comfort in simple things like music, books, and spending time with family.

I found it puzzling that the doctor and counsellor suggested such simple remedies for his severe condition. I questioned the doctor's decision to stop the medication and asked for more information about it. To my surprise, it turned out to be a relatively mild medication, slightly stronger than regular painkillers. I advised them to seek a second opinion from another doctor to help ease his suffering and make his remaining time more peaceful.

Thankfully, they listened to my suggestion and consulted another doctor who prescribed medication to alleviate his pain. Within a few hours, he passed away peacefully, surrounded by his loved ones. It was a bittersweet moment, as his suffering had finally come to an end, but the void he left behind was immeasurable.

The Pitfalls of Oversimplifying Psychosomatic Conditions

Doctors inquire about emotional well-being because many illnesses have both physical and psychological components. For example, chronic pain can result from physical injury as well as stress. If doctors only focus on the physical symptoms, they may overlook the psychological aspect, which can prevent the patient from receiving comprehensive treatment.

It is unfortunate that some doctors quickly attribute unexplained ailments to stress, as this oversimplification can be dangerous. There are numerous conditions with unknown origins, complex causes, or beyond the current understanding of medicine.

Even psychosomatic conditions, which have psychological roots, are real and can be just as debilitating as physical ailments. They are not confined to the mind and do not simply disappear on their own.

If you find yourself dealing with a perplexing medical condition that defies diagnosis, it is important to be persistent. Ask about the possibility of a psychosomatic cause and consider seeking a second opinion if the initial diagnosis falls short.

Do not let a doctor's simplified perspective hinder you from receiving proper treatment. Speak up for yourself and insist on proper care. Your health and happiness matter, and you deserve thorough attention.

9. Debunking Self-Help Books

In recent times, many individuals have become self-proclaimed motivation experts. Social media is flooded with numerous motivational videos featuring new gurus and their techniques every day. Surprisingly, these influencers have gained massive followings and attention.

Their success is mainly due to the support of those seeking quick fixes to improve their lives, covering aspects like work-life balance, relationships, and career growth. Social media provides an easy platform to create and share motivational content, leading to instant fame and influence. However, blind self-belief can be misleading, and even successful people may lack self-confidence. Insecurity can serve as a motivator for some.

Off-the-shelf modification programs can be risky. While they promise quick and easy results, they might be ineffective or even harmful. It's crucial to research and choose a program that suits your needs, as these programs can create unrealistic expectations and be too rigid, causing disappointment and discouragement.

The best way to enhance your life is to find a flexible program tailored to your individual needs. There's no one-size-fits-all solution – you need a program you can stick to that will help you achieve your goals.

Believe in Your Own Abilities: A Double-Edged Sword

"Believe in your own abilities, and you can do anything." This motivational phrase is often heard, but is it always a good thing to blindly believe in our own abilities? While self-reliance and confidence are generally positive traits that lead to personal growth and achievement, excessive belief in oneself can have negative consequences.

Let's examine the disadvantages of blind belief in one's abilities:

1. **Missing out on valuable insights:** By dismissing others' perspectives, a person may miss out on valuable insights, constructive criticism, or alternative approaches that could lead to better results.
2. **Limited personal and professional growth:** Believing that one knows everything and doesn't need others' help can limit one's potential for personal and professional growth.
3. **Isolation:** A person who constantly rejects others' opinions may find it difficult to associate with others, leading to isolation in personal and professional spheres.
4. **Poor decision-making:** Overconfidence can lead to bad decisions and negative consequences when faced with problems.
5. **Unnecessary stress**: Trying to do everything on one's own can lead to immense physical, mental, financial, and social stress.
6. **Missed opportunities for integration and innovation:** By not cooperating with others or seeking their help, a person may

miss opportunities for integration and innovative problem-solving.

7. Maintaining a false image: Constantly trying to maintain a perfect image can affect one's mental health when unable to meet expectations.

It's essential to strike a balance between self-confidence and humility. Accepting one's weaknesses and being willing to make changes is crucial for success in both personal and professional spheres. Seeking support from others and being open to their perspectives can lead to better outcomes.

Interestingly, many people who have achieved success lacked self-confidence. Their insecurity may have been a source of motivation, but it didn't stop them from seeking help and learning from others. In fact, research suggests that people with low self-confidence are more likely to engage in "mastery-oriented" behaviors, such as seeking feedback and putting in extra effort, which can lead to greater success.

While belief in one's abilities is important, it's equally important to recognize its limitations. Blind belief can lead to negative consequences, while humility and openness to others' perspectives can lead to greater success.

The Immense Power of the Mind: Separating Fact from Fiction

Exaggerated stories about willpower and the mind's potential often sell well. One such book I read when I was young had a line like this: "You can stop a speeding train with the power of your mind." However, the reality is that you cannot even stop a mosquito from biting you with your strong willpower.

The concept of the immense power of the mind is a complex and multifaceted topic that has been approached with caution and discretion by many philosophers, scientists, and spiritual leaders throughout history. Here are some reasons why this concept should be approached with discretion:

The mind has the power to create, to imagine, and to innovate, but it also has the power to destroy, to harm, and to deceive. The mind can be used to build up or tear down, to heal or to harm. Therefore, it is important to approach the concept of the immense power of the mind with caution and discretion, recognizing both its potential for good and its potential for harm.

The mind is not a static entity that can be easily defined or understood. It is a dynamic and constantly changing process that is influenced by a wide range of factors, including our thoughts, emotions, experiences, and environment. Therefore, it is important to approach the concept of the immense power of the mind with a recognition of its complexity and dynamic nature.

The mind is not a blank slate, but is shaped by a wide range of factors, including our culture, upbringing, and personal experiences. Therefore, it is important to approach the concept of the immense power of the mind with a recognition of the role that these factors play in shaping our thoughts, beliefs, and behaviors. The mind has the power to shape our perceptions and beliefs, but it can also be influenced by external factors such as media, social pressure, and cultural norms. Therefore, it is important to approach the concept of the immense power of the mind with a recognition of the potential for external influences to shape our thoughts and beliefs.

The concept of the immense power of the mind can be misused or distorted to justify harmful or unethical behaviors, such as manipulation, control, or exploitation. Therefore, it is important to approach this concept with a critical and discerning mindset, recognizing the potential for misuse and the need for ethical guidelines and safeguards.

Here are some examples of situations where willpower alone is not enough to achieve a goal:

1. **Addiction:** Willpower alone is often not enough to overcome addiction, as it can be a complex issue that involves physical, emotional, and psychological factors.
2. **Mental health conditions:** Mental health conditions such as depression, anxiety, and bipolar disorder can make it difficult to achieve goals, and willpower alone may not be enough to overcome them.
3. **Chronic illness:** Chronic illnesses such as diabetes, heart disease, and arthritis can make it challenging to achieve goals, and willpower alone may not be enough to manage symptoms and make lifestyle changes.
4. **Trauma:** Trauma can have a profound impact on a person's ability to achieve goals, and willpower alone may not be enough to overcome the emotional and psychological effects of trauma.

5. Learning disabilities: Learning disabilities such as dyslexia, ADHD, and autism can make it difficult to achieve academic and professional goals, and willpower alone may not be enough to overcome these challenges.

6. Financial constraints: Financial constraints can make it difficult to achieve goals, and willpower alone may not be enough to overcome financial obstacles.

7. Lack of resources: Lack of resources such as time, support, and access to information can make it difficult to achieve goals, and willpower alone may not be enough to overcome these challenges.

8. Social and cultural barriers: Social and cultural barriers such as discrimination, prejudice, and societal expectations can make it difficult to achieve goals, and willpower alone may not be enough to overcome these challenges.

9. Physical limitations: Physical limitations such as disabilities, chronic pain, and mobility issues can make it difficult to achieve goals, and willpower alone may not be enough to overcome these challenges.

10. Environmental factors: Environmental factors such as pollution, natural disasters, and political instability can make it difficult to achieve goals, and willpower alone may not be enough to overcome these challenges.

These are just a few examples of situations where willpower alone may not be enough to achieve a goal. It's important to recognize that achieving goals often requires a combination of factors, including willpower, resources, support, and external factors.

Is the Self-Improvement Industry Having a Negative Impact on You?

Let's Explore Some Aspects to Consider:

The self-improvement industry can be helpful, but it's important to be mindful of its potential impact on your life. Consider these points:

1. Make sure you're not spending too much time on self-improvement efforts. It's important to strike a balance between improving yourself and living your life.

2. Ensure your self-improvement efforts have a clear purpose and direction. It's important to know what you want to achieve and why.

3. Be aware of any tendency to constantly switch goals or lose focus. It's important to stay on track and not get distracted by new ideas or trends.

4. Be cautious of becoming too reliant on self-help programs and books. While they can be helpful, it's important to remember that personal growth is a lifelong journey and not a quick fix.

5. Remember that self-improvement is a journey, not a destination. Celebrate your progress, no matter how small, and appreciate where you are in your journey. Don't compare yourself to others or strive for perfection - it's unrealistic and can lead to disappointment.

6. Be aware of advertisements for self-help programs on platforms like YouTube. Some may use persuasive tactics to make you feel inadequate or pressure you into buying their products. Remember, you are not a failure, and you don't need to measure yourself against others.

Dr. Gregory Jantz, a mental health expert, recommends asking yourself some important questions to assess whether certain behaviors or activities are negatively impacting your life. These questions include:

1. Am I prioritizing this activity over other important aspects of my life?

2. Do I have control over these actions or behaviors?

3. Do I feel upset or distressed when I can't engage in these activities?

4. Does this activity consume a significant amount of my time?

5. Do I find myself spending more time on it than I initially planned?

6. Do I feel anxious or uneasy when I'm unable to do it or even think about not doing it?

7. Have certain automatic behaviors, like reading self-help books, started interfering with my life or relationships?

8. Despite my efforts to cut back or stop, do I keep returning to the same behaviors or activities?

Reflecting on these questions can help you identify areas that may require attention and support for a healthier and more balanced lifestyle. It's essential to be honest with yourself and consider these questions to ensure that certain behaviors or activities are not negatively impacting your well-being.

Overall, the self-improvement industry can be beneficial, but it's important to be mindful of its potential impact on your life. By striking a balance between self-improvement and living your life, being aware of potential pitfalls, and reflecting on your behaviors and activities, you can ensure that your journey towards personal growth is healthy and positive.

10. Each Man Is An Island

Do you find yourself constantly checking your phone throughout the day? You may be surprised to learn that, on a busy day, you may check your phone at least 80 times, and on an even more hectic day, this number can go up to 200 times. However, don't worry - there are apps available that can help you track and monitor your phone usage, allowing you to take control of your digital habits. Apps like AppTym, Quality Time, and App Usage provide statistics and insights into your phone usage patterns, while many Android and Apple phones now come with a default feature called "Digital Wellbeing" that offers similar information to help you effectively manage your screen time.

By using these apps, you can gain valuable insights into how frequently you unlock your screen and which apps you use most frequently. The data provided can include details such as the percentage of time spent on each app and the duration of usage. This awareness can help you make conscious decisions about your phone usage and potentially reduce excessive screen time.

The Dark Side of Phone Usage

The contemporary whirlwind of life has seamlessly integrated our phones into our daily routines. Whether for work or leisure, we instinctively reach for our smartphones. While using them for tasks like checking emails, using notepads, or accessing banking apps may appear benign, we must exercise caution, especially concerning our interactions with social media.

Throughout the pandemic, phone use soared as people found themselves with more spare time and limited alternatives for activities. Social media platforms such as Facebook, WhatsApp, Snapchat, Instagram, and Twitter have evolved into avenues for self-expression and connecting with others. Yet, excessive indulgence in social media can have detrimental effects on our well-being.

Certain individuals become so absorbed in social media that they dedicate substantial chunks of their day to posting, responding, and seeking validation through likes and comments. This perpetual need for attention and engagement can adversely affect their mental health and overall productivity. Even those in responsible positions often find themselves excessively posting, inadvertently neglecting other vital facets of their lives.

In the workplace, addiction to phones can hamper productivity and focus. As employees dedicate extensive periods to their devices, concerns arise regarding the attention allocated to actual work responsibilities. Similarly, when they return home, excessive phone use may compromise the quality of personal relationships and interactions with loved ones.

Negative comments and debates on social media platforms can contribute to stress, emotional turmoil, anxiety, and even arousal. This emotional weight doesn't only impact individuals but can extend to wider societal implications. Organizations should contemplate overseeing employees' social media engagement to ensure it doesn't interfere with their professional duties.

Furthermore, excessive phone usage can induce a feeling of detachment from the tangible world. Many people experience life vicariously through their phones, missing out on genuine human connections and authentic experiences. Engaging in mindless scrolling and focusing on others' lives instead of relishing our immediate surroundings can prove harmful to our mental well-being.

Even in social settings, we witness people engrossed in their phones, neglecting those in their immediate vicinity. This phone-centric behavior can impede meaningful conversations and create a rift among friends and colleagues. Instead of forging bonds and exchanging experiences, individuals often prioritize virtual connections with strangers.

Additionally, rampant phone usage has been linked to physical ailments such as "WhatsApp-itis," eye strain, neck and back discomfort, and even mental disturbances causing dizziness and insomnia.

To counterbalance the adverse consequences of phone usage, it's imperative to strike a balance between our digital and real lives. Practicing mindfulness in our phone habits and setting boundaries can aid us in regaining focus, enhancing relationships, and fostering a healthier lifestyle.

The Hazards of Using a Phone While Driving

Courts have ruled that using a phone in hands-free mode while driving is acceptable. However, many state police departments issue tickets for hands-free communication via Bluetooth while driving.

Who is right here

Our brains can handle only one task at a time, functioning via batch processing. While we can juggle multiple activities, our complete focus shifts from one task to another—multitasking is not within our brain's capability.

When talking on the phone while driving, the brain shifts attention between the ongoing conversation and driving. This constant toggling poses significant risks, as your focus divides between these two tasks.

Moreover, just because something is in our line of sight doesn't guarantee perception. Our brains must process information for us to truly see it. If your mental energy is invested in a phone conversation, you might not notice a child dashing in front of your car—an effect known as inattentional blindness.

A study by the National Highway Traffic Safety Administration revealed that a five-second distraction at 55 mph is like driving the length of a football field with closed eyes. Even a fleeting glance at your phone can have severe repercussions.

Attempting to pick up or dial a phone with your hands increases the accident risk by 95 percent. The government estimates that around 31% of road traffic accidents in India result from mobile phone usage while driving.

Globally, 1.4 million people lose their lives annually due to using phones while driving. Engaging with your phone behind the wheel could result in the demise of a responsible individual or leave a family without support.

Presently, it's common to view movies on your phone's dashboard while driving.

People rationalize this by claiming they only listen to the audio track, not watch the screen. However, even this constitutes a distraction and could lead to an accident.

The bottom line is that using a phone while driving carries immense danger. If necessity dictates phone use, it's imperative to pull over to a secure location first. Lives—both yours and others'—could hinge on such decisions.

The Dangers of Detox Myths

As a psychologist, I have witnessed firsthand the dangers of detox myths. Recently, two women came to my office, one with a history of mental illness and the other, her sister, an educated professional who had sacrificed much to support her. The first woman had been admitted to the ICU two weeks prior. Naturally, one might assume it was a suicide attempt, correct? However, the reality is different. She got an idea from somewhere that consuming large quantity of water could eliminate all the germs from her body and expel toxins. Accordingly, she drank a whopping 12 liters of water in a single day, as per her sister's account. (I find it hard to believe they drank that much water)

For if you ingest 5 liters of water at once, the outcome is certain: death. This is known as the lethal dose of water. After such excessive water consumption, essential minerals like sodium and potassium suddenly dropped in their bodies, leading to a loss of consciousness. (Hyponatremia, Hypokalemia)

Don't assume that this action is solely typical of someone dealing with mental health issues. This hazard takes on various forms and is present in multiple ideas. A type of thinking, wherein the notion that the entire body is toxic prevails, affects many individuals.

The idea that our bodies are filled with toxins is a popular belief, leading to the rise of detox diets and cleanses. However, experts agree that these claims are unfounded and misleading. Our bodies have natural detoxification processes, such as the kidneys, skin, and liver, which eliminate waste and toxins.

Understanding the concept of poison is crucial. Any substance can become harmful when consumed in excessive amounts, even natural substances like lemon juice. Similarly, some chemicals are beneficial to us, just as certain bacteria in our body play essential roles.

The notion that detoxing involves eliminating toxins through diets and cleansing processes is often based on misinformation. In reality, maintaining a balanced diet and regular exercise are the best ways to support our body's natural detoxification processes. Some chemicals can be harmful to us in small amounts, but others are beneficial. The same principle applies to bacteria. Our human body serves as a habitat to trillions of microbes, including bacteria, viruses, fungi, and various microorganisms. While the exact percentage varies, it is estimated that bacteria outnumber our own human cells in the body. Some estimates suggest that bacteria constitute about 1-3% of a person's total body weight.

As previously mentioned, our bodies have evolved sophisticated mechanisms and systems over millions of years. We possess specific organs like the kidneys and liver that work together to excrete waste and toxins as needed. With a balanced diet and regular exercise, these organs can perform their roles to maintain physical and mental health.

In conclusion, the evidence suggests that extreme detox measures offer little benefit and potentially serious risks. A lifestyle incorporating nutrition, exercise and stress management provides natural support for our in-built detox abilities. Rather than pursuing trendy quick-fixes, sustainable wellness practices nurture both body and mind. While some commercial interests promote detoxes, prioritizing established science-backed strategies usually leads to healthier outcomes. An integrated approach considering mind, body and lifestyle best promotes well-being.

Drinking Bitter Gourd Juice: Be Aware of the Risks

A quiz master on a Malayalam channel recently drank a glass of bitter gourd juice and claimed that he drinks four glasses of it every day. While bitter gourd is safe when cooked, its raw form contains natural insecticides that can be harmful in large quantities. Although some elements in bitter gourd can be used medicinally in small amounts, drinking raw bitter gourd juice can release harmful chemicals into the body.

Bitter gourd contains tetracyclic triterpenoid compounds called cucurbitacins, which are toxic and can cause vomiting, diarrhea, and even death if consumed in large amounts. Additionally, bitter gourd juice can interact with certain medications, so it's essential to consult a doctor before consuming it. The quiz master's advice to drink four glasses of bitter gourd juice a day is dangerous and could be harmful to one's health.

Bitter gourd is a healthy vegetable, but it's crucial to be aware of the dangers of pesticides often sprayed on it. In India, many farmers use pesticides that are not approved by the government or use them in excess, which can lead to the accumulation of harmful chemicals in the bitter gourd. To minimize the risk, it's important to wash bitter gourd thoroughly before consuming it and peel the skin, where most pesticides are concentrated. Proper cooking is also essential to ensure the vegetable is safe to eat.

While bitter gourd has health benefits, drinking raw bitter gourd juice can be risky. It's important to be aware of the potential dangers and take necessary precautions to ensure safe consumption.

The Risks of Consuming Medicinal Plants and Leaves

While some plants have health benefits when prepared properly, viewing all natural substances as inherently safe can be misguided. This perspective risks normalizing behaviors with serious health consequences. A wiser approach considers potential harms, encourages moderation and integrates traditional wisdom with scientific understanding.

For instance, daily consumption of neem leaves, long used to treat infections, can stress the liver if exceeding recommended amounts. Similarly, overindulging in tulsi leaves' antibacterial properties may burden the kidneys. Nature offers remedies, but also toxins - in excess, even "medicinal" plants damage vital organs over time.

Rather than believing nature intends our well-being, a balanced perspective recognizes its indifference. Plants serve ecological functions beyond human use. While traditional knowledge guides safe preparation and dosage, the notion that "natural equals harmless" neglects this nuance.

To make informed choices, consider both benefits and potential risks evidenced over time. Wisdom traditions understood nature's gifts within limits; modern lifestyles risk normalizing behaviors outside these. An integrated approach, incorporating science with care and moderation, better supports wellness through lifespans.

With education instead of fear, we make choices empowering healthy symbiosis with nature, not blind assumptions of unconditional safety. Moderation, preparation methods and ongoing research together safeguard traditional remedies' gifts within nature's balanced whole.

11. The Impact Of Body Language On Success

The idea that body language has a significant impact on success is a popular notion that has been perpetuated by various sources, including books, articles, and online courses. However, there is limited scientific evidence to support this claim.

Many studies that have found a correlation between body language and success have failed to establish a causal relationship. In other words, it's possible that success is causing the body language, rather than the other way around. Some studies have found no significant relationship between body language and success exist, while others have found mixed results.

Body language is not a fixed trait that can be easily measured or manipulated. People's body language can change depending on various factors, such as their mood, context, and cultural background. The impact of body language on success may depend on the context in which it is displayed. For example, certain body language cues may be more effective in some cultures or situations than others.

Some individuals believe that body language can reveal a person's level of confidence or nervousness. News outlets such as the Washington Post and Politico often analyze the body language of prominent figures after events like debates or meetings with world leaders. YouTube channels that claim to interpret body language have gained substantial popularity.

Law enforcement and government agencies utilize body language analysis to identify deception and understand true intentions. The University of Texas has found that experts train law enforcement and government personnel nationwide in the field of body language analysis.

While psychologists recognize that body language can convey emotions, many of their claims lack scientific evidence. For example, it is commonly believed that avoiding eye contact indicates lying, and rapid blinking suggests a lack of confidence. However, these notions are not supported by scientific research.

According to Professor Vincent Denault, a researcher from the University of Montreal in Canada, body language plays a significant role in politics. Politicians' gestures and movements greatly influence public perception. However, it is important to note that opinions from body language experts in the media may be intended for entertainment purposes and can lead to misconceptions.

The Use of Body Language Screening: A Questionable Practice

Despite the lack of scientific evidence, some consultants, specialists, career coaches, and airport screeners continue to use body language as a tool for assessing individuals. This practice has been criticized for its potential to incorrectly identify people as criminals or security threats. It is worrisome to consider how many people may have been wrongly accused or subjected to unnecessary scrutiny due to pseudoscientific body language screening. How many individuals have escaped airports only to commit crimes later?

Here are some examples of incidents where body language screening has gone wrong:

False positives: In 2010, a man was arrested at a security checkpoint in a US airport after a TSA officer detected a "suspicious" bulge in his pants. The man was carrying a large amount of cash and was mistakenly identified as a terrorist. It was later revealed that the bulge was caused by a medical condition and not a weapon.

False negatives: In 2018, a man was able to board a flight from Tokyo to Honolulu despite having a knife hidden in his carry-on bag. The TSA agent who screened him failed to notice the knife, which was later discovered by a flight attendant.

Racial bias: In 2014, a study found that TSA agents were more likely to target African American and Hispanic passengers for additional screening, even when controlling for other factors. This suggests that there may be racial bias in the way that body language screening is implemented.

Over-reliance on technology: In 2013, the TSA introduced the "Behavior Detection Program," which uses algorithms to identify passengers who may be a threat based on their body language and other behaviors. However, the program has been criticized for being overly reliant on technology and for failing to take into account the nuances of human behavior.

Lack of training: In 2019, a report found that TSA agents were not receiving adequate training in body language screening, which may lead to incorrect assumptions and missed threats.

Cultural differences: Body language can vary greatly across cultures, and what may be considered suspicious behavior in one culture may be considered normal in another. This can lead to misunderstandings and incorrect assumptions when screening passengers from different cultural backgrounds.

Medical conditions: Certain medical conditions, such as Parkinson's disease or multiple sclerosis, can cause individuals to exhibit unusual body language that may be misinterpreted as suspicious.

These examples highlight the limitations and potential pitfalls of body language screening. While it can be a useful tool in identifying potential threats, it should be used in conjunction with other methods, such as intelligence gathering and behavioral analysis, to ensure that the screening process is fair, effective, and unbiased.

Here are a few more examples where body language screening or interpretation may go wrong

1. Misinterpretation: A person might display nervous body language, such as fidgeting or avoiding eye contact, not necessarily because they are being deceptive, but due to anxiety or nervousness in certain situations.

Example: An individual might exhibit signs of nervousness during a job interview, leading an interviewer to assume they are hiding something, when, in reality, they are just anxious about the process.

2. Misinterpretation: Different cultures have varied norms regarding body language. What might be considered confident in one culture could be perceived as disrespectful in another.

Example: Direct eye contact is often seen as a sign of honesty and confidence in Western cultures, but in some Asian cultures, prolonged eye contact can be considered impolite or confrontational.

3. Misinterpretation: Introverted individuals may naturally exhibit closed body language, such as crossing arms or avoiding eye contact. This does not necessarily indicate deception but might be misconstrued as such.

Example: During a police investigation, an introverted suspect's reserved demeanor might lead investigators to suspect them of being untruthful, even if they are not.

4. Misinterpretation: Overanalyzing small gestures or movements can lead to false conclusions. A single gesture, taken out of context, may not accurately represent a person's true intentions.

Example: A person scratching their nose might be perceived as a sign of deception, but it could be due to an actual itch or a habitual behavior.

5. Misinterpretation: In high-stress situations, individuals may display atypical body language, making it challenging to accurately interpret their intentions.

Example: A witness to a traumatic event might exhibit erratic body language that could be misconstrued as dishonesty when, in reality, it is a result of extreme stress.

6. Misinterpretation: Certain medical conditions or medications can affect a person's body language, leading to misinterpretations.

Example: A person with a neurological condition that affects their facial expressions might appear untruthful even when they are telling the truth.

More body language myths

Clasping hands means resistance: This gesture may not necessarily indicate resistance, as it could be a sign of comfort, habit, or cold temperatures.

Avoiding eye contact means lying: Avoidance of eye contact doesn't always indicate dishonesty. Some people can maintain eye contact while lying, while others may avoid it due to shyness, cultural norms, or discomfort.

Reclining indicates lack of interest: Reclining may not necessarily suggest disinterest, as it could be due to various factors such as physical comfort, psychological state, or cultural norms.

Mirroring body language shows interest: The belief that mirroring someone's body language indicates interest is based on an innate human tendency to imitate others. However, this may not always be the case.

Lack of a smile indicates unfriendliness or dislike: People have different smiling habits due to personality, mentality, habits, or cultural norms. A lack of smiling doesn't necessarily indicate unfriendliness.

Touching face while talking indicates lying: While some studies suggest a link between face touching and lying, it's not a definitive indicator, as people may have various reasons for touching their face.

Lowered eyebrows indicate aggression: Lowered eyebrows can signal various emotions and cognitive states, including concentration, surprise, and confusion, not just aggression.

Body language is universal: This is a misconception, as body language is heavily influenced by cultural, social, and individual factors. Gestures considered respectful in one culture might be disrespectful in another.

Judging based on body language is flawed: Given the vast diversity in speech, style, and culture, making judgments solely based on body language is unreliable.

Variation in body language within small regions: Even in small areas like neighboring districts in Kerala, India, there can be significant differences in body language, highlighting its contextual nature.

Crossing your arms means you're closed off or defensive: Crossing your arms can simply mean you're feeling comfortable or relaxed. It's a common gesture that people use when they're feeling casual or laid-back.

Smiling means you're happy or friendly: Smiling can mean a variety of things, including anxiety, nervousness, or even aggression. It's important to consider the context and other facial expressions when interpreting a smile.

Fidgeting means you're nervous or anxious: Fidgeting can mean a variety of things, including boredom, excitement, or simply a lack of comfort. It's important to consider the context and other body language cues when interpreting fidgeting.

Standing up straight means you're confident or assertive: Standing up straight can simply mean you're feeling tall or powerful. It's also a common gesture when people are trying to make a good impression or project confidence.

Touching your face means you're lying or hiding something: Touching your face can simply mean you're feeling nervous or uncomfortable. It's also a common gesture when people are thinking deeply or trying to remember something.

Pointing with your feet means you're interested or attracted to someone: Pointing with your feet can simply mean you're pointing out something or indicating a direction. It's not a reliable indicator of interest or attraction.

Leaning in means you're interested or attracted to someone: Leaning in can simply mean you're trying to hear or see something better. It's also a common gesture when people are feeling friendly or trying to connect with someone.

Tapping your foot means you're impatient or anxious: Tapping your foot can simply mean you're feeling nervous or uncomfortable. It's also a common gesture when people are waiting for something or trying to release tension.

Steepling your fingers means you're confident or powerful: Steepling your fingers can simply mean you're feeling relaxed or comfortable. It's also a common gesture when people are thinking deeply or trying to concentrate.

The use of body language screening as a tool for assessing individuals is a questionable practice that requires further research to ensure its effectiveness and avoid potential harm. It's important to recognize the diversity and complexity of body language to avoid making incorrect assumptions and judgments.

12. The Secret Of "The Secret"

The Secret, authored by Rhonda Byrne, an Australian author and television producer, is perhaps the best-selling self-help book worldwide. The book claims that our thoughts can directly change our lives, and it has spent more than 190 weeks on the New York Times bestseller list. Books that have been translated into over fifty languages and sold more than 30 million copies are exceptionally rare in this world.

This "secret" gained prominence after appearing on The Oprah Winfrey Show and later being adapted into a movie. As of 2009, it has generated over $300 million in sales, making it an exceptional work without parallels. It is intriguing that despite being read by billions of people, it is still called "The Secret."

Rhonda Byrne's The Secret is considered an unscientific book for several reasons. Here are some of the problems with the book:

Rhonda Byrne's The Secret presents a magical technique suggesting the "Law of Attraction" to help people achieve their goals. Let's scientifically analyze the limitations of this highly celebrated book.

The Secret is based on the idea that positive thinking can attract positive experiences and outcomes, but there is no scientific evidence to support this claim. There have been no empirical studies that have proven a direct link between positive thinking and the manifestation of desired outcomes.

The book misinterprets the principles of quantum physics to support its claims. Quantum physics is a complex and highly mathematical field that has been misrepresented in popular culture, including in The Secret. The book's interpretation of quantum physics is not supported by scientific evidence.

Rhonda Byrne's understanding of the law of attraction is based on the idea that like attracts like, and that positive thoughts attract positive outcomes. However, this is a flawed understanding of the law of attraction, which is a concept that has been studied in psychology and sociology. The law of attraction does not imply that positive thoughts can manipulate the external world, but rather that like-minded individuals are attracted to each other. The book offers no scientific explanation for how positive thinking can attract positive outcomes. The book simply asserts that positive thinking works, without providing any empirical evidence or scientific explanation.

Rhonda Byrne suggests that individuals are responsible for their own experiences and outcomes, and that negative experiences are a result of negative thinking. This is a harmful and unscientific idea that blames individuals for their own misfortunes, rather than recognizing the role of external factors and systemic injustices. He conveniently ignores the role of external factors, such as systemic injustices, poverty, and discrimination, in shaping individuals' experiences and outcomes. The book suggests that positive thinking can overcome any obstacle, which is not supported by scientific evidence.

The Secret promotes a victim-blaming culture by suggesting that individuals are responsible for their own experiences and outcomes. This can lead to blaming victims for their own suffering, rather than recognizing the role of systemic injustices and external factors. The book simplify human psychology by suggesting that positive thinking can overcome any negative thought or experience. Human psychology is complex, and individuals' thoughts and behaviors are influenced by a wide range of factors, including their environment, upbringing, and life experiences.

The Secret ignores the role of privilege in shaping individuals' experiences and outcomes. Privilege, including white privilege, class privilege, and other forms of privilege, plays a significant role in determining individuals' access to resources, opportunities, and outcomes. It promotes a culture of entitlement by suggesting that individuals are entitled to a certain outcome or experience simply because they think positively. This can lead to unrealistic expectations and a sense of entitlement that is not supported by scientific evidence

The Secret is an unscientific book that lacks empirical evidence, misinterprets quantum physics, and promotes a flawed understanding of the law of attraction. The book ignores the role of external factors, promotes a victim-blaming culture, lacks a nuanced understanding of human psychology, ignores the role of privilege, and fosters a culture of entitlement. It's important to note that while "The Secret" has gained popularity, it has also faced significant backlash and criticism, particularly from the scientific and skeptical communities.

Individuals are encouraged to approach the book with a critical mindset and consider alternative perspectives.

Part II.
Rational Reverie: Unravelling History, People And Events Through Logical Dissection

13. Those Who Rewrote The Popular Equations Of Success

1. Shah Rukh Khan

Many of you may have heard the story of Maradona, who arrived in Hollywood with just $35 in his pocket. Similarly, when India's most admired actor, Shah Rukh Khan, first came to Mumbai, he had just ₹1500 in his hand, aspiring to earn at least one lakh rupees in total.

Let us take a look at some accidental events that happened in his life and how they changed his life radically. Shah Rukh Khan's father, Mir Taj Muhammad Khan, was a freedom fighter from Peshawar and an admirer of Abdul Ghaffar Khan, actively involved in the Indian National Congress. He was related to Major General Shah Nawaz Khan, a prominent officer of the Indian National Army. Shah Rukh grew up in the Rajendra Nagar area of New Delhi. His father owned several businesses, including a restaurant. Shah Rukh studied at the famous St. Columba's School in Central Delhi, where he even won the school's highest award, the Wall of Honour.

Between 1985 and 1988, Khan attended Hansraj College, where he studied economics. However, he spent a significant amount of time with the Theater Action Group (TAG) in Delhi, studying acting under the guidance of theater director Barry John. After completing his degree at Hansraj, SRK began studying for a Masters in Mass Communication at Jamia Millia Islamia University, but he eventually dropped out to focus on acting.

In his later life, Shah Rukh Khan faced unfortunate events. His father succumbed to cancer in 1981, and at 16, Shah Rukh found himself at a crossroads. As they brought his father's body home from the hospital, he looked at his crying mother. To add to his grief, his driver declared, "I will not take the car until the salary is paid." Ultimately, the teenager drove the car for the first time along the streets of Delhi with his father's body.

First of all, he did not initially set out to pursue a career in cinema. Shah Rukh Khan's entry into acting was somewhat accidental. While he was initially passionate about sports and pursued it with determination, a shoulder injury forced him to give up his sporting dreams. Subsequently, Shah Rukh joined the Delhi Theater Action Group (TAG). In 1988, he got the lead role in Lekh Tandon's television series "Dil Dariya," but its production faced delays. However, it was in 1989, with the TV series "Fauji" directed by Raj Kumar Kapoor, that he started gaining attention.

Initially, his ambitions were modest, aiming to work in serials and earn a living. We often hear advice from motivational speakers that to reach the top of a tress, you must at least aim for the sky and take the leap. Dealing with unruly hair, Shah Rukh had to resort to adjusting it with glue and water due to a lack of funds for hair gel. During his wedding, he even wore a rented coat from film sites. At that time, entering the cinema wasn't on Shah Rukh's mind, and his wife Gauri was also against that. He turned down many opportunities that came his way. The fact was that he wasn't particularly interested in the pulp nature of

Bollywood movies.

When he tried to get an opportunity in movies, it was not easy. Despite Shah Rukh's friend and film producer, Vivek Baswani, knocking on many doors for him, no director was interested in him. Even when he got the initial break, he wasn't an obedient guy waiting for chances, pleasing the seniors. Shah Rukh insisted on reading and listening to the script before committing to act even during his early days. Hesitating to display excessive humility around seniors in the industry, the young man was naturally deemed as arrogant.

Reflecting on his success, Shahrukh himself said, "People's success starts when they are in the right place, at the right time, with the right people." Yes, Shah Rukh Khan's success is a blend of coincidences and numerous random, unplanned factors. It was a time when the legendary Amitabh Bachchan took a break from the movies. The influential Aamir Khan and Salman Khan were touted by the media as successors to Amitabh Bachchan. But randomness proved that Shah Rukh was the third Khan to be the next king of Bollywood.

The irony is that, unlike the other two Khans, Shahrukh ventured into the movie industry without any godfather or other support. When personality is also taken into consideration, Salman and Amir were undoubtedly more handsome than Shah Rukh.

Shahrukh garnered attention by portraying anti-hero roles instead of the conventional leading roles associated with goodness. Perhaps that was enough to put an end to an actor's career. With growth came controversies and conflicts with his friends. The intimate scene in "Maya Memsaab" was celebrated by the paparazzi media; he was defamed as a womanizer. Shahrukh mistakenly believed that a journalist named Keith was behind it. Shah Rukh threatened to kill him, leading to his arrest by the police. In the police station, the inspector allowed him to make a phone call at the station, but Shah Rukh made that phone call to Keith himself, once again threatening him. These acts were more than enough to end his career fully. But it did not happen like that. Later, it turned out that another media worker was behind all these rumors.

In 1995, Shahrukh's profile underwent a transformation. His iconic collaboration with Yash Raj Film - "Dilwale Dulhania Le Jayenge" (DDLJ), was a turning point not just in his life but also in the history of the entire Indian film industry.

Even this association had the favor of randomness favoring him. When Shahrukh heard the story of DDLJ, he vehemently said no to it. He believed the character was not suitable for him in any way. He even confided in his friends that acting in this film might spell the end of his career. Despite being offered the role of Raj in DDLJ four times, he turned it down, stating that he was no longer young enough for a chocolate hero.

Shah Rukh had made up his mind that romantic movies were clichéd and desired to continue as a distinct type of actor. Aditya Chopra, the director of DDLJ, persistently tried to persuade Shah Rukh to take on the lead role. When all attempts failed, Yash Chopra, the patriarch of Bollywood and Aditya's father, personally intervened to convince Shahrukh to act in his son's movie. Yash Chopra told Shahrukh that he could not thrive in the industry without embracing romantic roles. Reluctantly, Shahrukh accepted the offer, partly due to his respect for Yash Raj.

Released in 1995, DDLJ became the longest-running film in theaters in the history of Indian movies. It marked the commencement of the Shah Rukh era as the "King of Romance" in Bollywood. Maratha Mandir, the single-screen cinema hall in Mumbai, has been screening Shah Rukh's Dilwale Dulhania Le Jayenge ever since its release in 1995. The cinema hall still sees many hardcore SRK fans watching the film with as much love and adulation. Even companies that used to feature heroines in their advertisements started featuring Shah Rukh.

During this period, some of Shah Rukh's well-received films faced setbacks in India, but movies like "Dil Se" gained recognition abroad. Around the same time, Hrithik Roshan, the son of director Rakesh Roshan, made his entry into Bollywood and received an overwhelming reception from the audience all around India. He became the most appreciated hero overnight when the movie "Kaho Na Pyaar Hai" was released. Many speculated that the Khan era in cinema was drawing to a close.

However, as Hrithik Roshan himself put it, "I am like a mushroom that suddenly sprouted when it rained." Yes, what he said was true. The Khans will stay consistently for a long time. Hrithik's unparalleled masculine beauty couldn't replace or overshadow any Khan in the industry.

The Mumbai underworld has been a hub of violence for decades. Here are some of the most prominent cases:

Gulshan Kumar: The founder of the T-Series music label was fatally shot by members of the Bombay underworld in 1997. Kumar, a wealthy businessman, had garnered enemies within the underworld. He was shot multiple times outside his Mumbai home.

Jyotirmay Dey: A journalist for the Mid-Day newspaper, Dey was assassinated by members of the Dawood Ibrahim gang in 2011. Dey had extensively covered the underworld, and his killing was interpreted as a warning to other journalists.

Pradeep Jain: The owner of the well-known Parasrampuriya Group of Companies, Jain was murdered by the Chhota Rajan gang in 1995. Jain was a rival of Rajan, and his death aimed to solidify Rajan's influence.

Rakesh Maria: The former Mumbai Police Commissioner and head of the anti-terrorist squad, Maria survived a bombing by the Dawood Ibrahim gang in 2003. The bombing aimed to eliminate Maria, who was viewed as a threat to the gang.

Jatin-Lalit's Father:

The father of music composers Jatin-Lalit was kidnapped and murdered by the underworld in 1997. The motive behind the killing remains unknown.

Laxman Rao Kirloskar: A notable businessman, Kirloskar was abducted and killed by the Dawood Ibrahim gang in 2002. Kirloskar's death was a caution to other businessmen who resisted paying protection money to the gang.

These are just a few instances of violence within Mumbai's underworld. The violence has profoundly impacted the city, serving as a reminder of the underworld's potency.

Despite facing persecution from right-wing extremists, Shah Rukh Khan remains the most revered Indian actor globally. In the 2023 TIME100 poll, Shah Rukh Khan garnered an impressive 4 percent of the 1.2 million votes cast by readers, further solidifying his worldwide popularity and influence.

Notably, his charisma and appeal extend beyond countries of Indian heritage, including Russia, China, Korea, and Japan, where he continues to enthral audiences and inspire admiration.

Despite his international acclaim and widespread adoration, Shah Rukh Khan has also encountered challenges and criticism, particularly from right-wing extremists. Nevertheless, his resilience and commitment to his craft have only bolstered his stature as an iconic figure in the film industry and a beacon of hope and inspiration for millions of fans worldwide.

2. Life of Indira Gandhi

Indira Gandhi's ascension to the post of Prime Minister of India was the result of a complex series of political events, strategies, and contingencies.

The first significant event that set the stage for her rise was the death of Jawaharlal Nehru in 1964. Nehru's passing created a significant void in Indian politics, as he had been the Prime Minister since India's independence in 1947. In the Congress party, Morarji Desai held the position of number two.

In the early 1960s, Morarji Desai wielded significant influence within the Congress Party, serving as a right-leaning, pro-business conservative leader. His stance positioned him as the opposing force to the left-leaning, liberal Nehru. As the finance minister in Nehru's government, Desai's influence grew to the extent that many considered him Nehru's natural successor. Nehru's decision to exclude him from the Cabinet in 1963 prevented Desai from automatically becoming the next Prime Minister. Consequently, after Nehru's death in 1964, Lal Bahadur Shastri assumed the role instead.

However, after Nehru's death, Lal Bahadur Shastri, Nehru's favorite, assumed the role of Prime Minister, and Indira Gandhi was appointed as the Minister of Information and Broadcasting in his cabinet.

Nineteen months later, the Syndicate and Desai found themselves in another power struggle. Initially considering Kamaraj as their candidate, the Syndicate shifted focus to Jawaharlal Nehru's daughter, Indira Gandhi, when Kamaraj declined the nomination.

However, tragedy struck again in January 1966, shortly after signing a peace treaty with Pakistan following the Indo-Pakistani War. Lal Bahadur Shastri died in Tashkent, Uzbekistan. This unexpected event left a void in the Prime Minister's office. Heated discussions arose regarding who would succeed him. At first, the Syndicate While Morarji Desai was a natural choice for many, the powerful Congress syndicate, comprising former Madras Chief Minister K. Kamaraj, Andhra leader Sanjiva Reddy, Mysore Chief Minister Nijalingappa, and

Bengal Congress Committee President Atulya Ghosh, tried to rally their support behind Kamaraj himself, but this was quickly abandoned when Kamaraj refused to be nominated saying he wasn't someone the country to unite behind. "No English, no Hindi. How?".

In the past two years, Indira Gandhi's political career faced uncertainty. Despite being widely recognized in Indian politics and having international acclaim, her strengths worked against her when Lal Bahadur Shastri became the Prime Minister. Shastri acknowledged the need for Mrs. Gandhi's support but didn't want to empower her as a potential challenger. Although he appointed her as the Information and Broadcasting Minister, he kept her somewhat distant. The tensions between them increased in 1964-65, and it's likely that Shastri was thinking of removing her from the Cabinet before his sudden death. Frustrated with her stagnant career, Mrs. Gandhi even considered leaving New Delhi and moving to England for a few years.

When Shastri passed away, Kamaraj started thinking about another person to become the Prime Minister. So, they chose Jawaharlal Nehru's daughter, Indira Gandhi, for the position. This choice by the Congress syndicate was a significant moment in Indian politics. It led to Indira Gandhi becoming the first woman Prime Minister of India. Her journey to power showed not only her political skills but also how various circumstances and alliances played a vital role in shaping Indian history. Kamaraj believed that the Syndicate could control Indira Gandhi through Congress committees and institutions, which they dominated. With widespread endorsements and support, Mrs. Gandhi became a formidable contender against Desai.

Upon hearing the news of Indira Gandhi's promotion as Prime Minister, socialist leader Ram Manohar Lohia referred to her as "Gungi Gudiya" (mute doll). Many blindly accepted his remark, which carried a tone of disdain. The main reason for this was Indira's lack of self-confidence in the early days. She was so nervous when she spoke. Leaders like Ram Manohar Lohia, Nath Pai, and Veenu Masani took every opportunity to mock and criticize any mistakes she made. At times, she was even discouraged from speaking, and Indira faced a hard time answering questions from the opposition. She used to feel nervous, sweat, and rub her hands when giving a speech. Not only the opposition but also leaders within the Congress, such as Morarji Desai, exerted pressure on her.

The transformation

After the 1967 elections, Indira underwent a remarkable transformation. She traveled 3,600 miles, addressing the people with much determination and vigor, becoming synonymous with strength and resolve. The countless experiences and interactions with millions of people completely changed her shyness and insecurity.

During an election campaign rally in Bhubaneswar, an unexpected turn of events unfolded as some individuals began hurling stones at Prime Minister Indira Gandhi. Despite the chaos, she refused to pause her speech. Ignoring the pleas of security personnel and party workers urging her to leave the venue, she pressed on with her address.

Initially unaware that she had been wounded, the crowd looked on as her nose began to bleed. Indira, undeterred, requested some ice, but none was available. Resourcefully, she reached into her handbag, retrieved a handkerchief, and wiped away the blood herself. Turning to the unruly crowd, she defiantly questioned, "Would you vote for such stone-pelting hooligans?" She boldly asserted, "This is not only a disgrace to me but also to the country." Indira Gandhi's resilience and poise in the face of adversity became a defining moment, showcasing her unwavering commitment to her convictions.

Indira Gandhi's staunch adversaries, far from breaking her spirit, fueled her determination. She fearlessly implemented pivotal measures that proved advantageous for the nation, notably the nationalization of crucial sectors, encompassing the takeover of eight banks. Bestowed with the moniker "Iron Lady" of Indian politics, she would later be likened to the formidable goddess Durga by Atal Bihari Bajpai. Indira Gandhi ascended to the zenith of political power, earning accolades as the formidable "Iron Woman" of contemporary times.

Some Crucial Factors of the Indo-Pak War (1971)

The then head of the Pakistan Military and government, General Yahya Khan, believed that India, ruled by such a weak woman, could be easily subjugated. However, Indira Gandhi's subsequent actions led to the division of Pakistan into two pieces. Let us look at some pivotal decisions that paved the way for this.

In a high-ranking meeting held by the Prime Minister, the Indian Army Chief, General Sam Manek Shah, disapproved of Indira's decision to attack Pakistan suddenly. He asserted that attacking Pakistan at this time would prove detrimental.

Indira was not pleased with her general's decision. After the meeting, she asked the general to stay back. General Sam Manekshaw thought he was going to be sacked, and he offered his resignation. But Indira asked why he was insisting that the war should be postponed.

He explained, "Madam Prime Minister, there is not much time left before the monsoon arrives in Bengal, a time when the Brahmaputra river swells significantly. Invading East Pakistan during this time would be a suicide attempt."

General Sam Manek Shaw was familiar with history's lessons on how harsh winters had decimated invading forces when Napoleon and Hitler invaded Russia. He explained that attacking in winter would minimize the Chinese army's ability to cross the extreme cold of the Himalayas. Indira had to accept this proposal. Time later proved his prediction to be accurate. The monsoon that followed was unprecedented, causing significant flooding in East Pakistan.

During this waiting period, Indira wasn't sitting idle. While her military commanders prepared for war, she personally met with leaders of the world's leading countries. Through interviews and engagements, she conveyed the message that India did not seek this war, and it was Pakistan who initiated the provocation.

By the end of the monsoon, India was prepared for war on the border, while Pakistan was not as well-prepared. India, however, remained steadfast in its policy of not initiating the attack. Indira understood that if India were to attack Pakistan, it might not receive widespread international support.

On the other side, General Yahya's overconfidence prompted him for a preemptive air strike launched on India's strategic areas such as Srinagar, Avantipur, Pathankot, Uttarlai, Jodhpur, Ambala, and Agra.

During that period, the United States was aligned with Pakistan. They attempted to sway many countries, including China, towards India, but the USSR warned that any Chinese attack on India would result in an attack on China's Shim Kyang province. The USSR also deployed troops along the Chinese border, causing China to withdraw its support. Arab countries sided with Pakistan.

Subsequently, the United States and Britain moved to directly aid Pakistan. They exerted pressure within the United Nations, leading to a temporary ceasefire forced upon India. Some speculate they were using this time to deploy troops to the Indian border. However, the Soviet Union vetoed these resolutions. US President Nixon ordered the movement of the 7th Fleet, led by aircraft carriers, towards the Bay of Bengal. This fleet, consisting of 13 warships and a nuclear submarine, moved to the Indian shore. While they briefly stopped at the port of Singapore for fuel and supplies, the Soviet Union had informed Indira Gandhi about these movements.

Indira Gandhi conveyed a bold message to American President Nixon. She said, "Mr. President, while it is within your authority to send battleships to India, I would be deciding whether those crossing my country's border should be allowed to proceed, be destroyed, or be returned." Britain's HMS Eagle also moved toward India. When both Britain and America attempted to threaten India from different sides, the Soviet Union's 10th operative battle unit was deployed to India. This formidable force included submarines, cruiser ships, and aircraft carriers.

Despite opposition from Arab countries, China, America, Britain, and even Sri Lanka, they were all scared of the Soviet Union. Consequently, America and Britain retreated, just as they had come.

It is even said by certain historians that the USA conspired with China to drop an atomic bomb in India. But experts warned that such an action may infuriate the USSR, which may retaliate with another atomic weapon in China or even the USA. The rest is history. In just thirteen days, Pakistan surrendered unconditionally to the Indian Army. Thereby, a new country, Bangladesh, was carved out of Pakistan.

Days When Indian Democracy Was Suffocated

The Emergency, a dark period in the history of democratic India, left an indelible stain that can never be erased or forgotten. It lasted for 21 months, from 1975 to 1977, when Prime Minister Indira Gandhi declared a state of emergency across the country. This chapter stands as one of the most controversial episodes in independent India's history. Let's take a closer look at the events leading up to and following the emergency:

Raj Narain, who had lost to Indira Gandhi in the 1971 parliamentary elections, filed a petition in the Allahabad High Court challenging her victory and alleging electoral irregularities.

The High Court found Indira Gandhi guilty of using government resources for her campaign and invalidated her election. Additionally, she was disqualified from holding any elected office for a period of six years.

Indira Gandhi appealed the High Court's decision to the Supreme Court, which granted a conditional stay on the verdict. This allowed her to retain her status as a Member of Parliament but revoked her right to vote in Parliament until the case was resolved.

The Allahabad verdict sparked widespread protests and strikes across the nation. Opposition leaders, notably Jayaprakash Narayan (JP), called for Indira's resignation and led unprecedented protests. Narayan urged the police, army, and law enforcement agencies to refuse to obey the government. This situation posed a significant threat to national security and public order.

Acting on Indira Gandhi's advice, President Fakhruddin Ali Ahmed declared a state of Emergency, citing "internal disturbances." This declaration granted the central government sweeping powers and temporarily restricted civil liberties.

Opposition leaders and critics were extensively arrested and imprisoned. Prominent figures like Jayaprakash Narayan, Morarji Desai, Atal Bihari Vajpayee, L.K. Advani, and others were taken into custody. The media's voice was silenced, further suppressing dissenting voices.

Indira's second son, Sanjay Gandhi, who had been on the outskirts of power until then, suddenly assumed full control. Indira's government was mocked as a kitchen cabinet. Under Sanjay's leadership, forced sterilization and slum clearance projects were executed as part of population control measures. People were manhandled, many died of infections, and numerous individuals left the cities. Slums were ruthlessly demolished.

However, on January 18, 1977, to the surprise of many, Indira Gandhi lifted the Emergency, announced elections, and released political prisoners. The Emergency officially concluded on March 21, 1977.

In the subsequent election, the public's anger over the Emergency found its expression, resulting in the resounding defeat of Indira Gandhi and the Congress party. Opposition parties united under the banner of the Janata Party to assume power.

Indira's Epic Comeback

There was a time when people harbored deep animosity towards Indira Gandhi. Initially, she was idolized, with the slogan "India means Indira, and Indira means India" being chanted. However, this sentiment quickly turned sour. Her name became associated with bitterness as her posters were defaced with charcoal smears and people even spat on them.

It seemed like Indira Gandhi's political career was coming to a permanent end. Her adversaries celebrated, believing her influence had been completely diminished. It appeared that Nehru's daughter had no chance of making a comeback in the minds of the people. This was a hopeless time not only for Indira but also for the Congress party.

However, a decision she made changed the course of her political journey. Her visit to Belchi, a village in Bihar, in August 1977 was a turning point that revitalized her political career and shaped the future of India.

Belchi, a small village in Bihar, was the site of a horrific incident of caste-based discrimination. The region was plagued by intense caste conflicts and severe social inequality. On the night of July 25, 1977, at least eleven Dalits were brutally burned alive by landlords belonging to the upper caste. Investigations later revealed that these individuals had been shot before their bodies were set on fire.

Despite the gravity of the situation, this incident received limited media coverage and the response from both the state and central governments was slow and inadequate.

The remote location of Belchi and the challenging monsoon conditions at the time contributed to this lackluster reaction.

In a bold move, Indira Gandhi decided to visit Belchi. This seemingly unlikely journey, however, had a profound impact on Indian politics. It was a game-changer not only for Indira Gandhi herself but for the entire nation.

The news of her trip shook the political landscape of India. The media gave significant importance to this decision of Indira. It is important to note that the protests against the Emergency were gaining momentum in Bihar. Additionally, in the subsequent elections, under the regional political leadership of Bihar, Indira Gandhi and the Congress party suffered a heavy defeat.

Despite repeated warnings from Congress supporters about the impassable swamp-covered terrain of Belchi, Indira Gandhi responded resolutely, saying, "What can happen?" For her, it was a do-or-die situation.

As her plane touched down in Patna, the air was filled with chants of "Indira Go back." She faced the crowd with her captivating smile. Gradually, the strength and frequency of those cries diminished, eventually giving way to slogans in support of Indira.

The journey to Belchi continued, with another 15 km to go. As expected, the car's tires sank into the swamp. They switched to large four-wheel jeeps, but even those vehicles couldn't travel much farther on the muddy road. The group found themselves stuck in the mud. The Congress leaders and security personnel urged Indira to abandon the plan, but for her, there was no turning back.

After some discussions with the local people, a farm tractor was brought to the site to pull the stuck jeep out of the slush. However, even the tractor eventually came to a halt. It seemed like the journey had come to an end. But Indira Gandhi was determined. She stepped out of the vehicle and started walking.

Someone from the crowd sarcastically suggested, "Why don't you travel on the back of an elephant?"

Many laughed at this remark. However, to everyone's surprise, Indira requested an elephant. An elephant was brought to the site. No one believed that the 60-plus-year-old Indira, who had been raised like a princess, would actually travel on an elephant. But to everyone's astonishment, she climbed onto the elephant without hesitation, claiming it was something she had always wanted to do. Spectators shouted, "Indira Gandhi Ki Jai!"

Indira Gandhi's arrival in Belchi was met with a reverent welcome. Some kneeled before her. To them, she was not just another political figure; she was seen as a deity who had come to their rescue. It was a moment of realization that only Indira could be their savior. Her return to the public eye created a sensation in the media, within Indian politics, and, most importantly, in the hearts of the people.

Decisions That Cost Many Lives

The Khalistan movement, the Blue Star operation at the Golden Temple, and the anti-Sikh riots—all these events not only altered Indira Gandhi's life but also shaped the future of India. In the late 1970s, it is widely believed that Jarnail Singh Bhindranwale was utilized by Indira Gandhi's Congress party to divide the Sikh vote and weaken its primary rival, the Akali Dal in Punjab. As Kuldeep Nayyar pointed out, Congress endorsed candidates supported by Bhindranwala. Furthermore, former Indian president Giani Zail Singh, Sanjay Gandhi, and others also provided support to Bhindranwala, as detailed in the book "Beyond the Lines" by Kuldeep Nayyar.

Contrary to everyone's expectations, Indira and India witnessed Bhindranwala transforming into a dangerous extremist. In his autobiography "Through The Corridors of Power - An Insider's Story," Dr. PC Alexander mentioned that after all the herculean efforts made by the Indira administration to tame him failed, Operation Blue Star was launched.

However, the first strategic mistake was that the government failed to take the necessary steps to prevent Bhindranwala from seeking refuge in the Golden Temple, a place of immense significance for Sikhs. Alternatively, Indira Gandhi's Intelligence wing could have cajoled him for a discussion and jailed him. Or he could have been assassinated in the way Mossad—the Israeli spy organization seeks revenge. Had Bhindranwala been assassinated, numerous lives could have been spared, and the revered Sikh temple might not have met destruction.

Was there an attempt to do that? Yes. Operation Sundown was the code name for a secret plan by India's external intelligence agency, Research & Analysis Wing (R&AW). The plan involved the Special Group, an ultra-secretive armed unit of the R&AW, attempting to abduct Sikh extremist leader Jarnail Singh Bhindranwale from Guru Nanak Niwas in the Golden Temple complex, Amritsar.

Rehearsals for the operation were conducted at the base, but it never took place due to the rejection by then Prime Minister Indira Gandhi. Instead, other options like negotiations were considered. However, these negotiations failed, leading to a worsening law and order situation in Punjab.

The details of Operation Sundown came to light almost three decades later, in January 2014, when India Today Magazine investigated the UK's declassified Top Secret documents. The last remaining militants either surrendered or were killed by June 10. While the army initially placed the total casualties at 554 militants and civilians dead, 83 troops dead (4 officers, 79 soldiers), and 236 wounded among government forces, other estimates peg the number of casualties as much higher.

After the Blue Star operation, militants assassinated Arun Shridhar Vaidya and attempted to kill Lt General Kuldip Singh Brar.

After the Blue Star operation, several Indian intelligence agencies such as RAW, IB, Military Intelligence, and the USSR intelligence agency KGB, along with numerous individuals, repeatedly urged Indira Gandhi to ensure that members of the Sikh community were not included in the Prime Minister's security forces. However, Indira never suspected such a threat. She believed in the principle of a secular nation and refused to discriminate against any community. Unfortunately, her unwavering faith had devastating consequences. It not only cost her own life but also led to the massacre of Sikhs. Government estimates suggest that around 2,800 Sikhs were killed in Delhi and 3,350 nationwide, while independent sources estimate the death toll to be between 8,000 and 17,000.

3. Rajiv Gandhi

Rajiv Gandhi's life serves as a testament to the significant role that unplanned, random, and fortunate events can have in shaping one's journey. He began his career as a regular pilot at Air India, finding contentment in his job and enjoying a peaceful life with his wife and children. His aspirations were modest, with his highest ambition being to fly between Delhi and Bombay.

However, life had other plans in store for him. The unexpected loss of his brother, Sanjay Gandhi, who was being groomed as Indira Gandhi's political successor, brought an unforeseen twist. Shortly after, Rajiv found himself thrust into a position he had never anticipated—a position he had no desire for. His wife, Sonia, struggled to come to terms with this unplanned entry into the political arena, a realm Rajiv had previously vowed to avoid.

Rajiv's journey was marked by a series of events that were far from planned. His empathetic nature led him to support the Sri Lankan Tamils, a cause he cared deeply about. He extended Military training by Indian Army training for the militant group fighting for the Tamil cause-The LTTE. This decision was the onset of setting the stage for a chain of unexpected consequences. During a visit to one of these training camps, little did Rajiv know that a woman named Tanu, present there, would later become the one to end his life. Rajiv Gandhi the then prime Minister decided to send a peace keeping army to Sri Lanka.

The IPKF was deployed in Sri Lanka in 1987 as a result of the Indo-Sri Lankan Accord, aiming to enforce a ceasefire and disarm militant groups, including the LTTE. The LTTE, led by Velupillai Prabhakaran, was initially in favor of the Indo-Sri Lankan Accord but turned against the IPKF as disagreements arose over the implementation of the accord. The LTTE resisted disarmament attempts by the IPKF and engaged in hostilities against them. The IPKF's military operations, sometimes in densely populated civilian areas, resulted in civilian casualties, leading to resentment among the Tamil population.

Human rights abuses, including allegations against the IPKF, further strained relations with the local population.

In Colombo, Rajiv narrowly escaped danger during a guard of honor when a Tamil assailant aimed a gun at him. Luck seemed to be on his side that day, allowing him to evade the perilous situation.

As time passed, Rajiv Gandhi's hold on power weakened, resulting in his loss in the 1989 election and the subsequent takeover of VP Singh as Prime Minister. In 1990, the Indian government made the decision to withdraw the IPKF from Sri Lanka. However, VP Singh stepped down during the election campaign, leading to an unforeseen turn of events for Rajiv Gandhi.

During the campaign, Rajiv Gandhi's statement that he would send more Indian troops to Sri Lanka if he returned as Prime Minister instilled fear among the Sri Lankan Tamils. This fear became the catalyst for the LTTE, a powerful terrorist group, to devise a plan to eliminate him. Despite warnings from intelligence agencies advising him against participating in election rallies in Tamil Nadu, Rajiv chose to disregard these cautions.

At an election rally in Sri Perumpattur, Tamil Nadu, Rajiv Gandhi encountered Tanu, a woman from the training camp he had inaugurated in Madras. She approached him with a garland of flowers, but a female inspector intervened, unknowingly altering the course of events. However, Rajiv Gandhi insisted that the lady sub-inspector allow Tanu to garland him, unknowingly inviting his own demise.

These events not only emphasize the role of chance, randomness, and unexpected turns in Rajiv's life but also serve as a reminder that even the most well-planned strategies can be disrupted by the unscripted nature of reality. Within this intricate tapestry of experiences, Rajiv's life became a testament to the unpredictable nature of fate. It demonstrates that decisions made with clear and noble intentions can have profound and unforeseen consequences in the future.

4. Rise of AR Rahman

Who is the most renowned music director in India? The answer is undoubtedly AR Rahman. He stands as the first Indian music director to win both an Oscar and a Golden Globe, an unparalleled achievement.

Was AR Rahman readily accepted by the Indian music industry merely because of his lineage as a musician's son, or because of his exceptional talent? Rahman served as a keyboardist for many famous and well-established music directors, including Ilayaraja and Ouseppachan. However, he was not recommended by any of these individuals based on his talent.

Let's delve into the string of random, unplanned events that paved the way for AR Rahman's rise as the most valuable name in the Indian music industry.

AR Rahman's entry into the film industry had a remarkably serendipitous trajectory. At that time, K. Balachander held a prominent position in the Tamil film industry and had entrusted Ilayaraja, the maestro of south Indian music, with his film's music creations. The K Balachander-Ilayaraja association created many evergreen hits.

However, a minor rift between Ilayaraja and K Balachander led to the unexpected end of their cherished partnership, paving the way for AR Rahman's entry into the Tamil movie industry. Maragathamani, a follower of Ilayaraja, replaced Ilayaraja and employed AR Rahman for the job. The choice of AR Rahman over Ilayaraja for "Roja" was just a result of a minor rivalry between K Balachander and Ilayaraja

This replacement provided an opportunity for AR Rahman, who embraced it as a trial. With the release of "Roja" in 1992, AR Rahman's captivating music flowed through the veins of India.

Rahman's film career began in 1992 when he started Panchathan Record Inn, a state-of-the-art recording and mixing studio in his backyard. It quickly became the most advanced recording studio in India and one of the most sophisticated and high-tech studios in Asia.

The following year, Rahman received the National Film Awards (Silver Lotus) award for Best Music Director at the National Film Awards for his work on Roja. The film's score was both critically and commercially successful, with its innovative theme "Chinna Chinna Aasai" becoming a hit across different languages throughout India.

AR Rahman's journey to success was shaped by a series of unplanned and unexpected events. One notable event was the difference of opinion between Ilayaraja and K Balachander, which led to a search for a new music director. This collaboration ultimately resulted in the partnership between Mani Ratnam and Kavithalayaa. One might wonder – if this conflict had not arisen, would AR Rahman's exceptional talents have gone unnoticed by the world? The twists of fate and the intricacies of chance have indeed woven a captivating narrative around AR Rahman's illustrious career.

14. Think About It For A Moment

The world is filled with infinite uncertainties and possibilities. Throughout history, some events have surprised us by changing unexpectedly. When we reflect on these changes today, we may mistakenly assume that the same outcomes would have happened even if certain events hadn't occurred. However, time follows its own course, and there are no restrictions on significant problems for humanity.

Even small changes in dramatic events, such as decisions made by leaders or the conditions of certain days, could have had a profound impact on history. Imagine if just a single factor had been different; the entire course of history could have been radically altered. This method of analysis, known as "What Ifs" (WHAT IFs), allows us to explore parallel possibilities that could have shaped history.

Had some minor alterations taken place in the world, the entire history and mankind would have changed. We, as a race, are the result of billions of random events that conspired together. In the theory of evolution, we call it natural selection. But in history, we never know what the outcomes would have been if a different twist had taken place. It's fascinating to contemplate the alternative paths history could have taken. Let's analyze some intriguing events through this approach.

The immediate event that led to the outbreak of the First World War took place on June 28, 1914. On that day, Archduke Franz Ferdinand, heir to the Austrian throne, and his wife

Sophie, Duchess of Hohenberg, were shot dead by a young Serbian nationalist of the Black Hand at Sarajevo, the Bosnian capital.

Austria accused Serbia of being responsible for the murder. In an effort to investigate the crime and hold those accountable, Austria-Hungary demanded punitive measures from Serbia and issued an ultimatum. However, Serbia did not fully comply, leading Austria-Hungary to declare war against Serbia on July 28, 1914.

As a protector of Serbia, Russia mobilized its army to respond to Austria-Hungary's attack. Germany supported Austria-Hungary in the war against Russia and announced their alliance. This series of military and defensive alliances set off a chain reaction, causing various countries to take sides and participate in the war. As the war progressed, the world witnessed countries joining one side or the other, and it evolved into World War.

Could have been a better world if...

What if Archduke Ferdinand had survived the assassination attempt in Sarajevo and managed to escape? If Serbia had chosen to yield to Austria's demands rather than rejecting them, the course of history could have been dramatically different. This decision could have prevented the outbreak of World War I, avoiding the escalation of tensions and hostilities that led to immense suffering and the loss of millions of lives.

The absence of the war might have influenced subsequent events, potentially preventing the rise of extremist ideologies, the Holocaust, and the establishment of Israel. The Austro-Hungarian Empire, renowned for its tolerance, would have continued as a model of coexistence, and the infamous Gulags under Stalin in the Eastern Bloc might never have come into existence. Great Britain would have maintained its global influence.

This scenario serves as a powerful reminder of how crucial decisions during pivotal moments in history can have profound consequences for the future of the world.

What Ifs of the Second World War

After World War I, Germany's alliances were shattered, and it seemed that no immediate assistance would be forthcoming from any other parties. The country was left to face the aftermath of the war largely on its own, with little support from former allies. Contrary to everyone's belief, Germany did not collapse fully. In fact, Germany was undergoing a period of revival led by a strong military.

Hitler, during World War I, was just a soldier who lacked significant education or any talents or specialities of any kind. He wasn't even an original German citizen and had no experience in governance or any special physical attributes. Yet, defying all the formulas of success, Hitler became the all-powerful ruler of Germany within a short period.

In his early days, Hitler attempted to join many arts schools but faced rejection from everywhere. Some historians speculate that had he succeeded in getting an admission somewhere and could make a living out of any other profession, he might not have become the dictator we know him as today. Fate or random events conspired enough to make him a leader. As a jobless wandering guy, he could easily secure a position as a temporary daily wage soldier, often referred to as a "mercenary" during World War I. Hitler survived death in a blast and suffered only from temporary blindness due to a gas attack. He could have died or been injured, but fate had other plans. The war didn't deter the rise of the Nazi party or prevent the occurrence of World War II.

1938-Le Munich Agreement

In 1938, the Munich Agreement was held in Germany, where Germany, Italy, France, and Britain came together to create a policy of appeasement towards Germany's territorial demands. This event is considered a significant lead-up to the outbreak of World War II.

Adolf Hitler's Germany had annexed Austria in March 1938, and subsequently, he attempted to incorporate the Sudetenland, a region in Czechoslovakia, into German territory. The claim was based on the presence of ethnic Germans in these regions, which he argued justified their integration into Germany.

During the Munich Conference, world leaders hoped to prevent war by allowing Germany to claim the Sudetenland in exchange for Hitler's promise not to pursue further territorial demands. British Prime Minister Chamberlain famously referred to the agreement as "peace for our time," though

Winston Churchill later criticized it as an "unmitigated disaster."

Despite the temporary delay in the outbreak of war, Hitler's ambitions were not restrained, and Germany went on to invade the remaining parts of Czechoslovakia in March 1939.

The Munich Agreement is often seen as a failed attempt to appease Hitler and avoid war. It highlighted the failure of diplomatic efforts to curb Hitler's aggression and ultimately contributed to the escalation of hostilities leading to the outbreak of World War II. While the agreement allowed Hitler to gain territory without resistance, it also emboldened him to pursue further territorial expansion, leading to more significant consequences later on.

Later, Hitler ordered his generals to destroy Czechoslovakia. Feeling it was unfair, the German general sent a message to British Prime Minister Neville Chamberlain, stating, "We are prepared to arrest Hitler if Britain helps." However, Chamberlain's opinion was that Hitler was not such a troublemaker.

Operation Sea Lion

France, once perceived as invincible due to its powerful army. But it was easily conquered by Hitler's Nazi army. Hitler's next target was the vast British Empire. Operation Sea Lion was the code name for Nazi Germany's planned invasion of the United Kingdom, intended to occur during the Battle of Britain, nine months into the Second World War. Following the capitulation of France, Hitler hoped that the British government would accept his offer to end the war. Invasion was considered a last resort, to be employed only if all other options failed. However, Germany faced greater challenges than anticipated in conquering. Britain, primarily due to the strength of the British army. Had Germany emerged victorious in Operation Sea Lion and conquered Britain, it would have been a significant triumph for Hitler. Germany would have gained a secure base to exert influence in North Africa, the Middle East, and the Indian subcontinent. The British Empire would have suffered a severe blow, leading to a decline in British power and global influence. Many colonies and territories could have fallen under Axis control. The loss of Britain as an Allied base of operations would have profoundly affected the strategies of the United States and the Soviet Union against Germany. Without the need to allocate resources to Britain, Germany could have focused on invading the Soviet Union earlier and with greater force, potentially altering the course of the war on the Eastern Front.

If Germany had conquered Britain, their air supremacy over Europe would have persisted. This would have posed significant challenges for the Allies in attaining air superiority in later stages of the war and limited the effectiveness of their bombing campaigns.

American Interference

The involvement of the United States in the Second World War was a critical moment. Japan launched an attack on Pearl Harbor, the naval base, a strategic point of the United States in

Hawaii, without any provocation. If such a preemptive aggression had been avoided, it surely would have had a significant impact on the course of the war and subsequent developments in world history. Let's consider some possible scenarios:

After the attack on Pearl Harbor, Germany continued the war by declaring war on America without any proper reason. The US started actively participating in the Second World War, and the efforts of American soldiers in the fight against Nazi Germany were crucial. Their determination played a significant role in the Allied powers' victory.

If Japan had not attacked Pearl Harbor, they could have consolidated their regional gains and expanded their forces to other areas. The absence of American forces could have allowed Japan to gain control over parts of Southeast Asia, Pacific Islands, and some areas of China.

If Japan had not attacked Pearl Harbor, both America and Japan might have engaged in negotiations and possible treaties before resorting to the extreme measures of the atomic bombings in Hiroshima and Nagasaki. Avoiding these bombings would have saved the immediate lives of two hundred thousand people and prevented long-lasting human suffering. This, in essence, was the most critical aspect of the situation.

If Japan had not suffered defeat, it would have had the possibility to reassert its authority and influence in various sectors in Asia, including India.

Had Japan abstained from attacking Pearl Harbor and not dragged the USA into the world war, the absence of American military support could have significantly strengthened the Soviet forces. As a result, the outcome of the war in the Eastern Front could have witnessed a significant change, with a possibility of more extensive German occupation in Soviet territories and a shift in the balance of power in Europe.

In the context of the Second World War, the absence of American involvement could have had a profound impact on the global order following the war. The potential for German success before their eventual defeat was a real possibility.

If the Axis powers had emerged victorious, American influence in the world would have diminished, while Russia and England would have expanded their spheres of influence significantly.

Without direct American involvement, the responsibility of fighting against Nazi Germany would have primarily rested on Britain and the Soviet Union, the two major allied forces.

Furthermore, if Japan had chosen to attack the Soviet Union instead of launching the infamous attack on Pearl Harbor, it is conceivable that Japan would have redirected its forces from Europe to assist Germany. This would have had significant repercussions on the outcome of the Pacific War and opened up different possibilities for the future.

German-USSR Relationship

During the Second World War, if Germany had refrained from attacking the Soviet Union, both countries could have achieved significant gains independently. The formation of a Soviet-German alliance would have completely altered the course and outcome of the war.

Let's explore some potential scenarios and their consequences:

Adolf Hitler, the dictator of Germany, and Joseph Stalin, the supreme leader of the Soviet Union, had agreed not to invade each other under the Non-Aggression Pact. If this alliance had held, it could have prevented the brutal aggression of Nazi Germany against the Soviet Union's civilian population.

The absence of German aggression would have allowed the Soviet Union to concentrate its resources and strength on other fronts, potentially leading to a more robust resistance against European invasions and better defense of its territories. It would have enabled the Soviet Union to redirect its resources and military power to other fronts, potentially resulting in more decisive victories elsewhere. Additionally, it would have provided the Soviet Union with the ability to strategically retreat and regroup in different areas, increasing the chances of achieving significant victories.

The war on the Eastern Front, fought by the Soviet Union against Germany, was one of the most costly battles. Initially, the USSR displayed competent leadership and tactics that could have prevented significant losses and allowed for more effective resistance against Germany. However, Stalin's distrust of his generals led him to make crucial decisions himself, which ultimately had detrimental consequences. If Stalin had followed the advice of his generals and strategically retreated in 1940 or 1941, many lives could have been spared on the battlefield.

By refraining from invading the Soviet Union, Germany would have been able to divert more attention to controlling other territories and establishing centralized control outside the Soviet Union's reach. This could have allowed Germany to consolidate its Nazi regime or potentially alter the outcome of the Allies' invasion of Normandy.

Overall, the decision of whether or not to attack the Soviet Union had far-reaching implications for the war, including potential shifts in alliances, strategies, and the overall balance of power.

The Atomic Bomb

Let's explore some intriguing scenarios: What if Germany had successfully conducted nuclear research and developed atomic bombs before any other nation? Before the final victory in Europe in April 1945, Franklin D. Roosevelt passes away. According to the American succession structure, Vice President Harry S. Truman assumes the presidency of the United States. As an inexperienced vice president with limited power, Truman becomes the president who holds the authority to decide whether to employ atomic weapons against Japan.

Now, what if Stalin and the Soviet Union had been the first to develop the atomic bomb? This would have had a profound impact on world history. Although the Soviet Union was also engaged in the development of atomic weapons during World War II, they did not succeed until 1949.

While Nazi forces were on the verge of reaching and potentially conquering Moscow, Stalin might have considered utilizing the atomic bomb.

Stalin would not have hesitated to deploy atom bombs in cities like Berlin and other German urban centers. The Soviets were determined to fully capture Germany, and after the war, a significant portion of Central Europe fell under Stalin's control.

If the USSR had succeeded in testing and deploying an atomic bomb before the United States, it would have altered the dynamics of the Cold War. With a nuclear monopoly, the Soviet Union could have exerted greater control over Eastern Europe.

Hitler and Atom Bomb

Let's explore another unsettling scenario: What if nuclear weapons had been developed by Hitler's side during the Second World War? Hitler might have considered bombing major cities in the Soviet Union or elsewhere in the world, leading to unimaginable consequences.

It is important to recognize that historical events can have vastly different outcomes depending on the decisions made during critical periods. The world would have been dramatically altered if Nazi Germany had emerged victorious and further spread its fascist ideology.

Those Who Sought to Eliminate Hitler

July 20, 1944: The most renowned and significant assassination attempt on Hitler was orchestrated by Colonel Klaus von Stauffenberg and a group of high-ranking German military officers. They planted a bomb in a briefcase at Hitler's meeting in his Wolf's Lair headquarters in East Prussia. Although the bomb exploded, Hitler managed to escape with minor injuries. Unfortunately, the conspiracy ultimately failed, leading to the arrest and execution of many conspirators. The world still remains unaware of why the attempt did not succeed.

March 13, 1943: A group of German officers conspired to assassinate Hitler during his visit to the Eastern Front in Smolensk, Russia. They concealed a bomb in Hitler's plane, but due to a malfunction, it failed to detonate. However, the plot was later uncovered, and Hitler ordered the execution of many involved officers.

November 8, 1939: A carpenter named Georg Elser planted a bomb in the Burgerbräukeller beer hall in Munich, where Hitler was scheduled to deliver a speech. However, luck was on Hitler's side. He concluded his speech earlier than expected and left the stage. Moments later, the bomb exploded, causing the death of eight individuals and injuring many others, but Hitler emerged unscathed.

Other Attempts: Numerous lesser-known assassination attempts on Hitler took place during his time in power. Johann Georg Elser attempted to bomb Hitler in a Nazi meeting hall in 1939, while Maurice made an attempt during a parade with Hitler in 1938. These endeavors, alongside the efforts of other individuals, aimed to bring an end to Hitler's reign.

Had any of these attempts succeeded, it could have potentially saved the lives of fifty million people and prevented immeasurable destruction.

However, it is important to acknowledge that Hitler managed to survive all threats until he eventually took his own life in his bunker in Berlin on April 30, 1945.

The need of What ifs

Engaging in parallel historical analysis or conducting "what-if" scenarios allows us to consider how events might have unfolded if certain circumstances had been different. Such questions serve as thought experiments, helping us understand the impact of individual decisions and alternative paths. However, it is essential to remember that decisions were influenced by the prevailing circumstances of that time, including available information, technological advancements, physical well-being, political and social contexts, and numerous other factors.

Similar to a spectator watching a football game and remarking, "Lionel Messi couldn't have missed that goal," we now reflect on whether we would have acted differently in those circumstances and created a better world. Instead of carrying the burden of shame, we should learn from history and move forward with improved understanding.

We should not simply be passive observers of history; rather, we ought to learn from it and prevent the repetition of past mistakes by making conscious and informed decisions.

15. The Story Of Two Failed Prodigies

1. Christopher Langan

A popular American television quiz program called "One vs. Hundred" features a single individual challenging a group of 100 people. The show offers a grand prize of one million dollars to the person who can outsmart this formidable group. Christopher Langan, who has been hailed as the smartest man in America, served as the quizmaster for one episode. With an IQ of 195 (compared to the average IQ of 100 and Albert Einstein's IQ of 150), Langan was truly exceptional in terms of intelligence.

During the show, the TV presenter asked Langan if he believed exceptional intelligence was necessary to participate in programs like this. In response, Langan stated, "Exceptional intelligence can be a double-edged sword. Intellectual prodigies often ponder profound matters but may overlook trivial details."

Langan's life story is a remarkable one, resembling that of Albert Einstein in terms of extraordinary genius and IQ. As mentioned earlier, finding someone as brilliant as Einstein is no easy task. Langan exhibited signs of being a child prodigy, starting to speak at just six months old. By the age of three, he was already asking thought-provoking questions and challenging existing ideas. He consistently ranked first in school exams without needing extensive studying. During his teenage years, he independently delved into physics and engaged in deep discussions on philosophical subjects. Langan also showcased proficiency in French, Russian, philosophy, music, literature, and painting.

During the mentioned TV program, Langan demonstrated remarkable accuracy in answering all the questions. He made the prudent decision to exit the game after winning $250,000 to avoid potentially losing a significant portion of his earnings.

Now, let's delve deeper into the life of Christopher Langan. Born in San Francisco, America, in 1952, his early years were marked by hardship. His mother faced numerous challenges in raising their five children, and poverty was a constant presence in their household, resulting in frequent moves from one place to another. As a result, Langan had to switch schools often. However, his exceptional intelligence allowed him to excel in every new school and class. Despite the constant disruptions, Langan taught himself subjects such as physics, philosophy, Latin, and Greek. He even discovered and pointed out errors in various textbooks.

However, Langan faced difficulties when it came to social interactions. He often found himself in disagreements with peers, teachers, and authority figures, which hindered his pursuit of a college degree. Nonetheless, he managed to earn a diploma based on his own merits. Following this achievement, Langan was awarded two full scholarships - one to Reed College in Oregon and another to the University of Chicago. Initially choosing Reed College, he later regarded this decision as a "significant mistake."

It's possible that Langan didn't secure the scholarship due to his mother's inability to complete the required paperwork or allocate time for it.

Before enrolling at Montana State University, Langan worked as a firefighter for the Forest Service for 18 months. Subsequently, he undertook physically demanding roles such as construction work, cowboy duties, and serving as a forest ranger. For two decades, he worked as a bouncer on Long Island.

While he attempted to attend classes at Montana State University, he encountered challenges in doing so. Despite attending some classes, he was unable to obtain a degree from the institution due to financial constraints, distance, and lack of transportation. Over time, Langan began to feel that he possessed a deeper understanding than his professors, prompting him to discontinue his formal studies.

During his time as a bar bouncer, he used his nighttime hours to develop his "Model of the Universe," an independent interpretation addressing various unanswered questions about the natural world. However, Langan spent his life engaged in work that neither his mind nor body found conducive to scholarly pursuits, a fact that went unnoticed and unaddressed.

In 1999, E Square magazine discovered his article and featured him extensively, labeling him as the most influential person in America. This subsequently garnered attention for him, and Langan started appearing regularly in various television, radio, religious, and educational political discussions.

Nonetheless, there exists significant criticism regarding the assertion of Langan's intellectual superiority on a global scale. Let's delve into the reasons behind this skepticism.

Despite possessing a high IQ, Langan has not made noteworthy contributions in any academic domain. Some critics contend that his self-proclaimed brilliance lacks empirical support and concrete achievements.

Langan has put forward multiple claims and theories that experts classify as pseudoscientific. For instance, consider his "Cognitive-Theoretic Model of the Universe" (CTMU). This theory seeks to unite physics and cognitive science primarily through imagination, without substantial empirical backing.

Langan's self-promotion and arrogance have attracted criticism. He has also faced accusations of disregarding other intellectuals and failing to engage in meaningful dialogues with his peers.

Langan left Montana State University without completing his education there, and he hasn't pursued any formal education afterward. Some critics argue that his lack of structured training in specific fields might have restricted his capacity to make significant contributions in those areas.

2. William James Sidis

Who is the most intelligent individual ever to be born in the world? There can be multiple answers to this question. Given our emphasis on science, prominent figures like Albert Einstein, Isaac Newton, and Stephen Hawking often come to mind.

We've already come across the story of Christopher Langan, a man whose IQ surpasses even that of Albert Einstein.

Among the many lesser-known brilliant individuals, the most brilliant person in the world at one point was James William Sidis. Unfortunately, the world remains unfamiliar with the name William James Sidis, a remarkable intellect who stood even higher than Einstein in terms of intelligence quotient. He was more than just a prodigy; he possessed exceptional abilities in mathematics and linguistics.

Let's delve into his family background. His Jewish parents managed to escape Jewish persecution in Ukraine and subsequently immigrated to America. Sidis' mother graduated from the Boston University School of Medicine, while his father, Boris, a psychiatrist who authored numerous books and articles, made significant contributions to the field of psychology. He was also a proficient scholar in multiple languages.

By the age of eight, Sidis had taught himself eight languages, including Latin, Greek, French, Russian, German, Hebrew, Turkish, and Armenian. He even devised his own language, which he named "Vandergood."

William Sidis stands as a unique genius who coexisted with the likes of Nikola Tesla and Albert Einstein in America. Clearly, William's parents were no ordinary individuals. Possessing a wide array of qualities, they began educating their child within the first few months of his life. By the age of one, he could read letters, and some accounts suggest that by two years old, James was reading newspapers. Astonishingly, at just four years old, William read both the Iliad and the Odyssey, Greek epics, in their original language.

At six years old, he delved into the works of Aristotle, Plato, and others. This intellectual prodigy even penned his own scientific book about the human body at the tender age of four. By eight, he had mastered seven languages. Like many other prodigies, William excelled in multiple subjects, consistently ranking first in school exams by the age of nine.

This exceptional child not only brought immense pride to his parents but also became a tool for his father to validate his methodical publications within the academic world.

Eager to establish records in their son's name, the parents attempted to enroll William James at Harvard University when he was only 9 years old. However, their efforts were in vain, as the endeavor proved unsuccessful due to the boy's young age. Harvard officials cited emotional immaturity as the reason for their decision.

Thanks to the dedication and guidance of his father, psychologist Boris Sidis, William developed strong logical skills. This prowess enabled him to accomplish a unique feat: achieving a score of 254 on an IQ test, the highest ever recorded since the test's inception.

It's worth noting that Albert Einstein and Stephen Hawking had IQ scores of 160. The score required to join Mensa, a society comprising the top 2% of the population in terms of intelligence, is 148.

Without wasting time, his parents enrolled him in Tufts College. While there, William invested a significant amount of his time in identifying errors in mathematics textbooks and scrutinizing Einstein's theory of relativity.

Eventually, at the age of 11, his parents managed to secure his admission to Harvard. His exceptional academic performance continued at Harvard as well. Representatives from MIT in Boston likened him to Carl Friedrich Gauss and had no doubts about his potential to become one of the world's greatest mathematicians. Some even prophesied that William would become a defining figure in the field of astronomy. Remarkably, William graduated from one of the world's premier universities with a mathematics degree at the age of 16. Sidis authored "The Animate and the Inanimate," an exploration of his ideas about the origin of life, cosmology, and the potential reversibility of the second law of thermodynamics.

While young William enjoyed a comfortable existence within the protective embrace of his home and parents, his interactions with unfamiliar individuals in the outside world unveiled the limitations of the education imparted by Boris and Sarah Sidis.

Subsequently, William faced a series of failures. Forming friendships and engaging with people proved challenging for him. Between the ages of 11 and 16, his time at the university was demanding. He found himself spending most of his time alongside classmates who were at least twice his age. In the presence of journalists, he once shared, "I aspire to lead a flawless life. The only way to do so is to live in solitude. I have always harbored a disdain for crowds."

After graduating, William got an opportunity to teach at Rice University in Houston. However, he was disheartened by the attitude of his older students towards him. Naturally, his role as a 16-year-old teacher was met with skepticism from his fellow educators.

Meeting the expectations of parents and the press to deliver extraordinary results commensurate with his intelligence created a challenging experience for the young William. Struggling to navigate the jealousy of his colleagues compounded the difficulties he faced there.

By that time, he had already gained significant fame, although the university administration terminated his employment. Eight months later, he returned to Harvard to pursue law, but William dropped out a year before completing his degree. At the age of 20, he was arrested for participating in a socialist demonstration in Boston and served an 18-month prison sentence. With his father's intervention, he managed to avoid further incarceration and was rehabilitated at his father's psychiatric facility. This may have been an attempt by his father to guide his son back within the bounds of societal norms.

During a certain period, the press was fixated on him, racing to publish reports about the prodigy named William. This attention deeply bothered the introverted William, and he yearned to escape the commotion. Consequently, he wandered through various places under different aliases, engaging in various jobs. He readily undertook roles such as carpentry, stonework, and road paving.

Yet, people continued to identify him in numerous locations. Each time he was recognized, he would leave that job and relocate to different cities. This cycle persisted endlessly, while he concurrently penned books. He was in the process of writing a 1200-page book titled "The Tribes and the States." The book centered on the tribes of the American Northeast and the history of Native Americans up to the mid-19th century. Although Anpa began this work in 1935, William never managed to complete it. The manuscript was discovered unpublished after Sidis's passing. He authored this historical work under the pseudonym "John W. Shattuck."

William wrote several books on science and astronomy, all published under different names to keep his authorship concealed. Regrettably, none of these self-published books gained traction. He expended his savings pursuing this endeavor, yet after his death, a newspaper reporter uncovered these works. They were subsequently published by mainstream publishers, leading to a resurgence of Sidis's fame.

Neither women nor friendships were entirely familiar to William. But he formed a close bond with a woman named Martha Foley and engaged in a romantic relationship with her. However, it was later revealed that they became the subject of a newspaper article, which contained deeply personal and negative content about William. In 1944, William filed a lawsuit against the "New Yorker" magazine, alleging that it contained false information about his life. He received some monetary compensation through a settlement, but gradually, the world was beginning to forget him.

In that same year, at the age of forty-six, William Sidis passed away due to a cerebral hemorrhage. At the time of his death, he was holding a portrait of Martha Foley. Although they had been married to other individuals for a considerable period, William's feelings were unaffected. He loved in his own unique way, guided solely by his intelligence. Throughout his life, William Sidis remained distant from concepts of sex, art, music, and sentimentality.

While IQ can be an indicator of certain cognitive abilities, it is not the sole determinant of success in life. Success encompasses a wide range of factors beyond intellectual intelligence, including emotional intelligence, social skills, perseverance, adaptability, and personal contentment. The cases of William James Sidis and James Langan serve as a reminder that intelligence alone does not guarantee a successful or fulfilling life.

16. Yes, Our Story Is Heard

1. Abraham Lincoln

Abraham Lincoln, born in 1809, is widely regarded as one of the greatest figures in human history. As the 16th President of the United States, he is synonymous with the fight for equality and played a pivotal role in emancipating slaves within the nation. His journey was shaped by uncertainty, unforeseen events, and the whims of fate. Numerous random occurrences played a significant role in shaping his character and propelling him towards greatness.

Lincoln faced trials and setbacks in his early years. At the young age of 23 in 1832, he experienced the bitterness of unemployment, losing his job. Simultaneously, his aspirations to secure a seat in the State Legislature were met with the harsh reality of defeat. Challenges continued to arise. At 26, he suffered the heartbreaking loss of his lover, Ann Rutledge. At 29, he missed out on the coveted position of Speaker in the Illinois House of Representatives.

In 1848, at the age of 39, another blow came as his hopes of becoming the Commissioner of the General Land Office in D.C. were shattered. A decade later, at 49, his dream of becoming a U.S. Senator slipped through his fingers.

Despite personal, professional, and political troubles, Lincoln remained determined. In 1846, he was elected to the U.S. House of Representatives, where he made significant strides in the fight against slavery. This demonstrated his unwavering commitment to a greater goal, even in the face of challenges.

In 1861, at the age of 52, Abraham Lincoln reached the pinnacle of his political journey, assuming the esteemed role of President of the United States. His voyage was characterized by unwavering determination. Lincoln's face adorns the five-dollar bill, a symbol of his enduring influence on the nation he played a pivotal role in shaping.

Let us examine his story more closely:

Abraham Lincoln's story is not one of flawless victories. Destiny crafted Lincoln's life like a masterpiece with its share of chances and surprises. It was his resilience and determination that transformed it into art.

Lincoln's formal education was limited to a few months of schooling at a local log cabin school. He was largely self-taught and had to work hard to compensate for his lack of formal education.

His first business venture, a general store in New Salem, Illinois, ended in failure. It struggled to thrive, ultimately leading to its closure.

In 1834, Lincoln ran for a seat in the Illinois legislature but was defeated. However, he was eventually elected to the legislature in 1836, overcoming his initial setback.

Lincoln's first fiancée, Ann Rutledge, passed away from typhoid fever in 1835. Her death devastated Lincoln, and he expressed his grief through numerous poems and letters. Lincoln faced challenges in establishing himself as a successful lawyer in the early years of his career. He encountered setbacks and criticism for his lack of experience and his folksy, backwoods manner.

In 1854, Lincoln ran for a seat in the U.S. Senate but was defeated by Stephen Douglas. This setback was significant as Lincoln had hoped to use the Senate seat as a platform to speak out against slavery.

The death of Lincoln's mother, Nancy Hanks Lincoln, in 1849 was a profound loss for him as they were very close. Despite his best efforts, Lincoln was unable to prevent the secession of several Southern states and the outbreak of the Civil War. He felt a deep sense of responsibility for the failure to preserve the Union and the loss of life that ensued.

When Abraham Lincoln was assassinated at the age of 56, not only did a life come to a sudden end, but a triumph and a symbol of humanity also ceased to shine. Lincoln's assassination marked a tragic turning point in history, cutting short a journey characterized by resilience and leadership. His life represented more than just personal achievements; it stood as a beacon of hope and progress for humanity.

The path to fame, glory, and greatness for Abraham Lincoln was far from a straight line. Small changes could have made him an ordinary person. For instance, in the 1860 election, Lincoln faced formidable candidates, including Stephen Douglas, who had previously defeated him. If Lincoln had not emerged victorious, the Civil War might have been delayed or even avoided. Other presidents may have had a more conciliatory approach towards the South. Upon closer examination, we can identify numerous small factors that contributed to Lincoln's greatness.

2. Albert Einstein

Albert Einstein, born in 1879, is widely regarded as a towering figure in the realm of human intellect. However, his journey exemplifies the intricate interplay of chance, resilience, and the unexpected. Despite his eventual greatness, he faced notable setbacks along the way, showcasing the unpredictable nature of life.

Einstein encountered challenges from a young age. At the age of 4, he exhibited a lack of verbal expression, causing concern among those around him. Initially, he failed an entrance exam for a prestigious school. However, he was granted a second chance, which he successfully passed.

The loss of his father at a young age and his struggles in school added to his hardships. Eventually, he found employment at a patent office, where he authored papers that revolutionized the field of science. In 1905, he experienced a remarkable year, producing four pivotal papers. His exceptional contributions led to him being awarded the Nobel Prize in 1921.

Einstein's life was marked by unexpected events. He entered into matrimony twice, had a son, and was forced to flee Nazi Germany. Fortunately, he had a friend who aided him in his escape. Einstein spent the remainder of his life in the United States, dedicating himself to his work and advocating for peace.

What if Einstein had not faced failure in the entrance exam for the Swiss Federal Polytechnic School? His life's trajectory could have taken an entirely different course, potentially depriving the world of his ground-breaking contributions to physics.

What if Einstein had not encountered the mathematician who recognized his talent? Without a second chance to attend the Polytechnic School, his academic and scientific journey might have taken a different direction altogether.

What if Einstein had not accepted the position as a patent clerk? His time at the Patent Office provided him with the intellectual freedom to explore his scientific ideas, which ultimately led to his revolutionary discoveries.

What if Einstein's theories had not been confirmed through experiments? His work might have been relegated to mere speculation, denying the world the advancements in physics that his theories spurred.

What if Einstein had not managed to escape Nazi Germany? His remarkable intellect and advocacy for peace might have been silenced, robbing the world of his invaluable contributions to science and humanity.

Lastly, Albert Einstein's groundbreaking formula, $E=mc^2$, revolutionized the field of physics by demonstrating the interchangeability of mass and energy. This concept has had a profound impact on the world, leading to the development of nuclear power and the creation of atomic bombs. Unfortunately, the devastating power of these weapons was tragically demonstrated during World War II when the United

States dropped atomic bombs on the Japanese cities of Hiroshima and Nagasaki, resulting in the loss of hundreds of thousands of lives and swiftly bringing an end to the war.

3. Bill Gates

Bill Gates is a widely recognized name in the world of entrepreneurship. With a net worth of over $200 billion, he is undoubtedly one of the most successful individuals in this field. However, what if I were to inform you that his success was not solely attributed to his hard work and determination? In fact, chance, probabilities, unexpected events, randomness, and luck played a significant role in propelling him to the pinnacle of success.

Born in 1955 to a well-off family in Seattle, Washington, Gates had the privilege of a prosperous upbringing. His father, a successful attorney, and his mother, a philanthropist and university regent, provided a nurturing environment. At the age of 13, Gates displayed a keen interest in computer programming, embarking on the path to write his own software code.

What if he had not been exposed to programming at such a young age? Would he have still been able to achieve the entrepreneurial triumphs he enjoys today?

Gates attended Lakeside School, an exclusive private institution in Seattle, where he fortuitously crossed paths with his future business partner, Paul Allen. Sharing a mutual passion for computers, their partnership would prove to be a lifelong endeavor.

What if their meeting at Lakeside School had not transpired? Would their paths have intersected at a later stage, leading to the establishment of Microsoft?

In 1973, Gates enrolled at Harvard University. However, he made the audacious decision to drop out just two years later, redirecting his focus towards his software company, Microsoft. What if he had chosen to complete his degree? Would he have still pursued a career in software development?

In 1975, Gates and Allen founded Microsoft, with their initial product being a version of the BASIC programming language for the Altair 8800 microcomputer. The Altair's popularity at that time provided a platform for Gates' BASIC programming language to flourish. What if the Altair had not garnered such widespread popularity? Would Microsoft still have achieved the remarkable success it did?

During the early 1980s, Microsoft was approached by IBM to develop an operating system for their new personal computer. Gates and his team created MS-DOS, which became a pivotal achievement. What if IBM had chosen another company for this task? Would Microsoft have still emerged as the dominant force in the software industry?

In 1987, Microsoft went public, catapulting Gates into the ranks of the wealthiest individuals in the world. What if the company had chosen not to go public? Would Gates have achieved the same level of success he enjoys today?

In the 1990s, Microsoft faced legal challenges, including antitrust lawsuits alleging the company held a monopoly in the software industry. What if Microsoft had lost these lawsuits? Would the company have been able to maintain its industry dominance?

In the early stages of Microsoft, Bill Gates had the opportunity to take stricter measures against software piracy. However, he opted for a more lenient approach, allowing billions of individuals worldwide, including those in India, to learn and master Windows OS, Microsoft Office, and personal computers in general. This decision ultimately proved beneficial for Microsoft, as it created a larger pool of computer-literate individuals, fostering the growth of the company's business.

4. Charles Darwin

Charles Darwin, the renowned British naturalist, is widely recognized for his groundbreaking theory of evolution through natural selection, as presented in his seminal work "On the Origin of Species," published in 1859. This revolutionary concept transformed our understanding of the incredible diversity of life on Earth.

Born into a prosperous family in Shrewsbury, England, in 1809, Darwin's father was a successful physician, while his grandfather was a botanist. However, his early education was interrupted by illness, leading to his enrolment in a boarding school in Scotland. What if circumstances had prevented him from attending this school? Would he still have developed his profound interest in natural history?

In 1825, Darwin enrolled at the University of Edinburgh with the intention of studying medicine. However, he found the lectures unstimulating and lackluster. Consequently, he diverted his focus towards his true passion: natural history. Immersed in this field, he dedicated his time to collecting and studying specimens. What if he had never discovered his fervour for natural history? Would he still have pursued a career in science?

In 1827, Darwin's father sent him to Christ's College, Cambridge, to prepare for a career in the clergy. However, Darwin's unwavering passion for natural history persisted, and he devoted much of his time to studying and collecting specimens. What if circumstances had prevented him from attending Cambridge? Would he have still formulated his groundbreaking theory of evolution?

In 1831, Darwin seized the opportunity to join the HMS Beagle as a naturalist, embarking on a voyage that would take him around the world, particularly mapping the South American coastline. What if Darwin had not been selected for this expedition? What if he had not been born into a privileged family that afforded him such opportunities? What if he had not been fortunate enough to encounter the finches that later served as the cornerstone of his theory? Would he have still collected the crucial data that formed the foundation of his groundbreaking theory?

During his voyage on the Beagle, Darwin amassed a vast collection of specimens, including the now-famous Galapagos finches, commonly referred to as "Darwin's finches." These finches played a pivotal role in the development of his theory of evolution. What if he had not collected these finches? Would he have still formulated his influential theory?

Following the Beagle's return to England, Darwin dedicated several years to studying his collections and refining his ideas. In 1858, he commenced writing "On the Origin of Species," which was published the subsequent year. What if he had encountered obstacles preventing the publication of his book? Would his ground-breaking theory have garnered the recognition it deserved?

Unsurprisingly, Darwin's theory of evolution through natural selection faced considerable opposition and controversy from various quarters, including scientists and religious leaders. In 1871, he published "The Descent of Man," expanding his evolutionary theory to include humans. This publication, though controversial, solidified Darwin's position as one of the foremost scientists of the 19th century.

What if he had not written this influential book? Would his theory of evolution have been considered complete? What if he had lacked support from his friends and colleagues? Would his theory have gained acceptance?

5. Colonel Harland Sanders

Colonel Harland Sanders, the esteemed founder of Kentucky Fried Chicken (KFC), led a life filled with chance, probabilities, unexpected events, randomness, and luck. His path to becoming one of the most accomplished entrepreneurs in the fast-food industry was far from linear, punctuated by numerous "what if" scenarios that underscore the significance of these factors in his journey.

Sanders was born on September 9, 1890, in Henryville, Indiana. Tragically, his father, a railroad worker, passed away when Sanders was only five years old, leaving his mother to single-handedly raise him and his two siblings. What if Sanders' father had not died at such a young age? Would his upbringing and career trajectory have taken a different course?

After dropping out of school in the seventh grade, Sanders worked a series of odd jobs, including serving as a streetcar conductor, a farmhand, and a soldier in the U.S. Army during World War I. What if Sanders had not departed from his education? Would his career have followed a different path?

In 1930, Sanders inaugurated his first eatery, Sanders Court & Café, in Corbin, Kentucky. This establishment, encompassing a gas station, motel, and restaurant, swiftly gained popularity for its delectable fried chicken. What if Sanders had not chosen to open his restaurant in Corbin? Would he have achieved success in an alternative location?

In 1935, a devastating fire razed Sanders' restaurant, leaving him with nothing. Yet, he persevered, rebuilding the establishment and continuing to serve his renowned fried chicken. What if the fire had not ravaged his restaurant? Would Sanders have persisted with his fried chicken or transitioned to a different menu?

In 1952, Sanders ventured into franchising, enabling a group of entrepreneurs to establish the first KFC franchise in Utah.

What if Sanders had refrained from franchising his restaurant? Would KFC still have evolved into a prosperous fast-food chain?

In 1959, Sanders sold KFC to John Y. Brown Jr. and Jack C. Massey for a substantial sum of $2 million. What if Sanders had chosen not to sell KFC? Would he have continued to helm the company himself?

In 1964, Sanders assumed the role of a spokesperson for KFC, with his image becoming synonymous with the brand. What if Sanders had not become the face of KFC? Would the brand have achieved the same level of success?

Sanders passed away on December 16, 1980, at the remarkable age of 90. What if he had not lived such a long life? Would KFC have prospered without the guidance of its esteemed founder?

6. Elvis Presley

Elvis Presley, widely known as the "King of Rock and Roll," emerged as a musical icon whose journey was characterized by the unpredictability of chance, the twists of fate, and strokes of luck. Born in 1935 in Tupelo, Mississippi, his early years unfolded in relative obscurity. However, little did the world know that a series of serendipitous events would propel him to legendary status.

Elvis' passion for music blossomed at a young age, influenced by the captivating rhythms of gospel, blues, and country that surrounded him. His acquisition of a guitar at the age of 11 proved to be the catalyst for an unforeseen future. The melodies he played in his modest home ignited a flame that would revolutionize the music industry.

At 19, Elvis walked into Sun Records to record a song as a birthday gift for his mother. Unbeknownst to him, this seemingly mundane act would serve as a turning point. The owner of the studio, Sam Phillips, discerned something extraordinary in Elvis' voice—a fusion of styles that would redefine music. The decision to record that song became the thread that unraveled the tapestry of his destiny.

In 1954, when Elvis recorded his debut single, "That's All Right," chance intervened once again. A local radio DJ played the song, and the response was electrifying. This unexpected stroke of luck propelled Elvis into the spotlight, igniting a fervor among listeners that would shape the course of popular music.

The convergence of Elvis' magnetic stage presence and the advent of television further catapulted his career. His appearance on "The Ed Sullivan Show" in 1956 marked a historic moment. The ensuing frenzy among teenage fans earned him the moniker "Elvis the Pelvis," solidifying his status as a cultural phenomenon.

Elvis's family relocated to Memphis, Tennessee when he was a young boy. What if they had not made the move? Would Elvis still have discovered his passion for music? It is likely that he would have been exposed to music in some form, but Memphis, with its vibrant blues and rock and roll scene, truly nurtured Elvis's musical journey.

While Elvis's first single, "That's All Right," gained popularity in Memphis, it was his recording of "Heartbreak Hotel" that garnered national attention. What if he had not recorded that iconic song? Would he still have achieved fame as a singer? It is possible, but "Heartbreak Hotel" undeniably transformed Elvis's career.

Elvis's music was not without controversy. Many regarded him as a rebellious and provocative figure, leading to the banning of his songs on numerous radio stations. What if Elvis had not encountered such backlash? Would his music have been more widely embraced? It is plausible, yet the controversy surrounding his music undoubtedly contributed to his soaring popularity.

Elvis's life was also punctuated by unexpected events. In 1956, he was drafted into the army and served for two years. What if he had not been drafted? Would he have continued his musical pursuits or embarked on a different path? It is difficult to say, but it is evident that Elvis's time in the army had a profound impact on him, potentially influencing his musical evolution.

In 1967, Elvis married Priscilla Anne Beaulieu, and her presence played a significant role in his life. Elvis's life was also marked by struggles with addiction and health issues. What if he had not grappled with these challenges? It is possible that these struggles contributed to his untimely demise.

7. Henry Ford

Henry Ford, renowned for his role in the business world and philanthropy, is widely recognized for his significant impact on modern America and the industrial sector. His legacy extends beyond founding the Ford Motor Company, as he is also acclaimed for his charitable contributions.

Ford's life story exemplifies the interplay of chance, determination, and unforeseen circumstances that shape destinies. Born in 1863 on a Michigan farm, his journey unfolded amidst promising opportunities and unexpected twists. His upbringing fostered a fascination with machines and mechanics, laying the foundation for his future innovations. At the age of 16, Ford's decision to leave the farm and become a machine shop apprentice exposed him to new ideas and skills that proved pivotal in his later pursuits.

In 1896, Ford's curiosity and experimentation with gasoline engines led to the creation of his first automobile, the Quadricycle. This breakthrough was a direct result of his inquisitiveness and the mechanical knowledge gained during his formative years. Fortuitously, a group of investors provided financial support, propelling Ford into entrepreneurship and enabling him to realize his visionary aspirations.

As the Ford Motor Company took shape, another stroke of serendipity occurred in 1903 when the company was established with an initial investment of $28,000. One can only speculate how different history might have been if those investors had made different choices. These fortuitous beginnings intricately tied to chance moments shaped the trajectory of the automotive industry, leaving an indelible mark on the world.

In 1913, Ford revolutionized manufacturing with the introduction of the assembly line, a breakthrough inspired by his exposure to meatpacking processes and his relentless pursuit of efficiency. This innovation transformed not only the manufacturing landscape but also societal norms and the dynamics of the workforce.

Despite these positive aspects, historical records raise questions about Ford's alleged connections with the Nazi Party and Adolf Hitler during the 1930s. In 1938, Ford received the Grand Cross of the German Eagle, one of the highest Nazi decorations awarded to foreigners. While some argue that this was an acknowledgment of Ford's contributions to German industry, others see it as a tacit endorsement of Hitler's regime.

One of the most contentious aspects of Ford's legacy is his publication of anti-Semitic materials, particularly the distribution of "The International Jew," a collection of articles perpetuating harmful stereotypes. Although Ford later distanced himself from these writings, their impact was significant, and they were even cited by Hitler in "Mein Kampf."

Ford's leadership within his own company was marked by controversies. His authoritarian management style and resistance to change made him an unpopular chairman. His decision to continue producing the Model T, despite consumer demand for innovation, resulted in a decline in market share for Ford Motor Company.

The legacy of Henry Ford is undoubtedly complex. While he revolutionized the automotive industry and made philanthropic contributions, allegations of association with the Nazi Party and his controversial leadership at Ford Motor Company cast shadows on his reputation. It is crucial to examine historical figures with a nuanced perspective, recognizing both their positive contributions and the controversies that may define their legacies.

Henry Ford's life was a tapestry woven from chance, probability, unexpected events, and luck. He was a man shaped by his experiences, who seized the opportunities that came his way. While success might have still been possible without luck, it is undeniable that fortune played a significant role in Ford's journey.

8. J.K. Rowling

J.K. Rowling, the brilliant mind behind the enchanting Harry Potter series, emerged from a tapestry woven with threads of chance, resilience, and the ability to overcome failures. Her story exemplifies the unpredictable twists that life can take and the unexpected opportunities that arise.

Born in 1965, Rowling's early years were marked by adversity. She faced challenges such as a complex relationship with her father and her mother's battle with illness. At 17, in 1982, her application to Oxford University was rejected, leading her to the University of Exeter where she pursued studies in French and Classics. Little did she know that this decision would lay the foundation for her future success.

After her studies, she joined Amnesty International in London, further shaping her worldview and perspective. Chance encounters and experiences during this time contributed to her growth as a writer. In 1990, at 25, an idea sparked during a train delay, an idea that would give birth to the magical world of a young wizard. However, the passing of her mother soon after cast a shadow over her life. The timing of the idea for Harry Potter was crucial.

Her experiences at Amnesty International enriched her understanding of social issues, which she subtly wove into her stories. Struggling to find her voice amidst domestic difficulties, she managed to complete only three chapters of Harry Potter by age 38. Her move to Edinburgh in 1995 marked a turning point, propelling her towards completing the manuscript for the first book.

It wasn't until 1996 that the book found a home when Bloomsbury, a small London-based literary publisher, agreed to publish it, thanks to the owner's daughter urging them on. They provided a modest advance of £1500. In 1997, seven years after the concept of the young wizard was conceived, the first Harry Potter book was finally published.

By 2004, J.K. Rowling had achieved the remarkable feat of becoming the first author to reach billionaire status through her book writing, as reported by Forbes.

What if she had never been discovered by Bloomsbury, just like with every other publisher? J.K. Rowling might have faded into obscurity.

9. Marilyn Monroe

Marilyn Monroe, the legendary actress and model, was born on June 1, 1926, in Brooklyn, New York. Her early life was filled with hardships as her parents struggled with poverty and her father's mental illness, creating a tumultuous home environment. Perhaps influenced by her difficult childhood, Monroe sought refuge in the world of acting.

Monroe initially started her career as a model, posing for pin-up photos and taking on small roles in B-movies. What if she hadn't been discovered by a photographer? Her early work in modeling and bit parts helped her gain exposure and develop her skills.

In 1950, Monroe landed her breakthrough role in "The Asphalt Jungle," which proved to be a pivotal moment in her career, earning her critical acclaim and recognition. Her subsequent roles in "Gentlemen Prefer Blondes" and "How to Marry a Millionaire" solidified her status as a prominent Hollywood star, establishing her as both a leading lady and a sex symbol.

In 1954, Monroe married baseball legend Joe DiMaggio. Their marriage played a significant role in her life and career, bringing her a level of fame and attention that she may not have achieved otherwise.

However, Monroe's life was also marked by personal struggles, including addiction and mental health issues. These challenges may have influenced her acting and public image, endearing her to audiences and making her more relatable.

Tragically, Monroe passed away in 1962 at the age of 36 due to a barbiturate overdose. Her untimely death has since become an integral part of her legend and mystique, solidifying her status as an iconic figure in American cinema.

Overall, Marilyn Monroe's life and career were shaped by a combination of chance, unforeseen events, randomness, and luck. While she worked hard to pursue her dreams, there were numerous factors beyond her control that contributed to both her success and her tragic demise. What if she had been born in a different city or hadn't been discovered by a photographer? It's impossible to say for certain, but it's evident that Monroe's life was influenced by a complex interplay of fate and circumstance.

10. Mark Zuckerberg

The story of Facebook and Mark Zuckerberg highlights the importance of chance, unexpected events, twists of fate, randomness, and the "what if" factor. From his initial struggles to the massive success that revolutionized online connections and inspired the film "The Social Network," it demonstrates the unpredictable nature of life.

Today, Mark Zuckerberg is a well-known figure worldwide, but his journey began with challenges. Facebook, initially known as "thefacebook.com," brought him fame but also led to a legal battle with Cameron and Tyler Winklevoss and Divya Narenda. This unexpected lawsuit shaped his early entrepreneurial experiences and resulted in a surprising settlement: 1.2 million Facebook shares.

Before thefacebook.com, Zuckerberg's path took a significant turn that could have unfolded differently. His previous project, Facemash, relied on chance and probability by allowing students to rate photos for attractiveness. However, life's unpredictability intervened, causing controversy and Harvard University to shut down the project. Apologies and criticisms followed, marking an unexpected twist in his journey.

What if Zuckerberg hadn't faced the lawsuit? His focus might have remained undisturbed, potentially impacting the trajectory and pace of Facebook's growth. If Facemash hadn't sparked controversy, his path might have taken a different direction, influencing his perspective and approach to future projects. It is impossible to say with certainty, but it is evident that Zuckerberg's life and career have been shaped by a complex interplay of fate and circumstance. Considerations such as being born in a different country or era would undoubtedly have added further layers of influence.

11. Oprah Winfrey

Oprah Winfrey, a prominent figure in the media industry, is undeniably a symbol of triumph over adversity. She was born in 1954 in Kosciusko, Mississippi, and her early years were characterized by poverty and challenging family dynamics, which set the stage for her extraordinary journey.

Raised by her grandmother in poverty, Oprah's upbringing was far from ordinary. However, chance intervened when she moved in with her mother in Wisconsin at the age of six, introducing a half-sister into her life.

What if Oprah hadn't moved in with her mother? Her experiences might have taken a different path, drastically altering the course of her life.

At the age of 13, Oprah faced a pivotal moment when she ran away from home after enduring sexual molestation. Despite the trauma and difficulties, she faced, her unwavering determination helped her persevere through those dark days. Another unexpected turn of events occurred when she became a mother at the young age of 14, but tragically, her premature baby did not survive. This heart-breaking loss deepened her grief and sorrow.

However, instead of breaking her spirit, these experiences fortified her strength and resilience, enabling her to face future challenges with courage and determination.

At 17, winning a beauty pageant provided a glimmer of hope and led to an internship at a radio station, igniting her passion for media. As she pursued her career, setbacks continued to arise. While a job as a news anchor in Nashville was a stepping stone, a role in Baltimore was short-lived due to a producer's decision.

The story could have taken a different turn. If Oprah hadn't won the beauty pageant, her exposure to the media might have been delayed, potentially influencing the trajectory of her career.

In 1983, Oprah was drawn to Chicago, a city that would play a pivotal role in her path to success. Seizing a unique opportunity to take over a struggling talk show called "AM Chicago," she transformed it into the renowned and globally celebrated "Oprah Winfrey Show." Her remarkable resilience, combined with chance encounters and bold leaps of faith, paved the way for unparalleled success. Starting from a local platform, she eventually became a billionaire with immense global influence.

12. Richard Branson

Richard Branson, an esteemed English entrepreneur, is renowned for his incredible success in building the Virgin Group, a global conglomerate with diverse business interests. His path to success is marked by serendipitous encounters, unplanned ventures, and calculated risks that have made a lasting impact on the business world and beyond.

Despite facing challenges with dyslexia and leaving school at 16, Branson's determination and entrepreneurial spirit shone through from an early age. His decision to drop out of school unexpectedly led to the launch of his first business venture, a thriving magazine called "Student." This initial triumph fueled his ambition.

Branson's passion for music led him to establish a record store, which grew into the well-known chain known as Virgin Records. A spontaneous choice to sign the Sex Pistols to his record label proved to be a pivotal moment, catapulting both the band and Virgin Records to greater fame and success.

A fortuitous encounter at a party introduced Branson to Nik Powell, who became his business partner in founding a production company. This partnership expanded Branson's entrepreneurial horizons.

Branson's foray into the airline industry was not part of a predetermined plan. However, he recognized an opportunity to provide exceptional customer service, leading to the establishment of Virgin Atlantic. A near-fatal boating accident served as a stark reminder of the significance of taking calculated risks in his life and career.

In an unexpected turn of events, Branson ventured into the realm of space tourism by collaborating with Virgin Galactic to develop SpaceShipTwo, a commercial spacecraft with the potential to revolutionize space tourism. This unplanned project has become a significant part of his entrepreneurial legacy. Virgin Galactic's achievement of winning the $10 million X-Prize for developing a private spacecraft capable of reaching suborbital space solidified Branson's position as a pioneer in the field of space tourism.

An unforeseen partnership with British Airways played a crucial role in expanding Virgin Atlantic's reach in the airline industry. In 1999, Branson received an unexpected honor when he was knighted by the Queen for his contributions to entrepreneurship and philanthropy, recognizing his commitment to innovation and society.

Through a series of chance encounters, unplanned ventures, and calculated risks, Richard Branson has demonstrated that entrepreneurship is a journey filled with unforeseen opportunities and extraordinary accomplishments, leaving a lasting legacy that extends far beyond the business realm.

13. Soichiro Honda

Born in 1906, the journey of Soichiro Honda from a Japanese inventor to the founder of the monumental Honda Motor Company highlights the interplay of chance, unexpected events, and unwavering determination that shape destinies.

A fortuitous encounter with an auto repair shop set the course of his life. Six years of dedicated work honed his skills, laying the foundation for his future. However, what if he hadn't come across that repair shop? Could his path have taken a different direction?

Upon returning home, Honda's fortune led him to establish his own auto business, a seemingly arbitrary decision that became a stepping stone. The Great Depression of 1937, beyond his control, compelled Honda to pivot to Tokai Seiki, focusing on producing piston rings for Toyota. What if his designs had met the requirements immediately? Could that have altered the trajectory of his career?

Undeterred, Honda embraced the unexpected and learned from it. After two years, Toyota recognized his perseverance and rewarded him with a contract. This triumph was the result of chance and unwavering effort converging.

Twists and turns persisted, with war and calamity testing Honda's resolve. His indomitable spirit transformed adversity into opportunity, giving birth to Honda's motorcycle legacy.

What if those setbacks had defeated him? Could the world have missed out on his innovative contributions?

In the 1950s, Honda introduced the "Super Cub" motorcycle, a simple and affordable design that became a phenomenal success. Its popularity exceeded expectations, garnering global recognition.

Entering the U.S. motorcycle market in the 1960s faced skepticism, but the unexpected oil crisis boosted demand for their fuel-efficient motorcycles. The Honda Civic's success in the 1970s, driven by its reputation for reliability and fuel efficiency, aligned perfectly with market needs, establishing Honda as a reputable car manufacturer.

In the 1980s, the launch of the luxury brand Acura tapped into a different market segment, expanding Honda's business. The Honda Accord's accomplishments in the 1980s and 1990s, partly attributed to its reputation for reliability and fuel efficiency, brought fortuitous success to Honda and fostered a loyal customer base.

14. Steve Jobs

In the realm of business history, few stories captivate and inspire as much as that of Steve Jobs, the co-founder of Apple Inc. Born in 1955, his life's narrative is a testament to the unpredictable interplay of chance, unexpected events, and moments of sheer randomness that defied conventions and forever transformed his destiny.

From humble beginnings to billionaire status, from inventive genius to iconic entrepreneur, Steve Jobs' extraordinary journey serves as a masterclass in how serendipity and tenacity can shape not only an individual's life but also the trajectory of an entire industry and the world at large. Let us delve into the remarkable saga of Steve Jobs, where the unplanned, unforeseen, and fortuitous moments took center stage.

Right from the start, Jobs grappled with the whims of fate. His mother's decision to put him up for adoption set the stage for a blue-collar upbringing in Palo Alto, California. Adopted by Paul and Clara Jobs, he was introduced to electronics and mechanics at an early age, igniting his fascination with technology. This early exposure laid the foundation for his future innovations. What if his upbringing had been different? Would he still have become the tech visionary we know today?

As he embarked on higher education, Jobs chose an unconventional path. Instead of pursuing a traditional degree, he followed his interests, fueling his thirst for knowledge. His relentless curiosity eventually led him on global journeys, including an enlightening trip to India, where he explored Zen Buddhism. What if he had taken a more conventional academic route? Would his curiosity have found a different outlet?

In 1976, a momentous collision of chance and vision occurred when Jobs befriended Steve Wozniak, a brilliant engineer. Their complementary skills and shared passion for technology led to the creation of Apple. Together, they co-founded Apple Computers.

Jobs' visit to Xerox PARC exposed him to the graphical user interface (GUI) and mouse-driven navigation, which inspired the development of the Macintosh and revolutionized personal computing. Apple faced early struggles, and the uncertainty of success marked their journey. What if their first product hadn't gained traction? Could Apple have ventured into a different realm of innovation?

However, challenges emerged. A pivotal decision in 1983, marked by the seemingly random appointment of John Sculley, proved disastrous for Jobs, leading to his ousting from the company he had founded.

Following his departure from Apple, Jobs founded NeXT, focusing on computer platform development. While NeXT's hardware fell short of expectations, its software innovations laid the groundwork for future Apple products. This adversity-driven determination allowed NeXT to thrive even as Apple faced financial difficulties.

Then came another twist: Apple's acquisition of NeXT in 1997, marking Jobs' return. What if Apple had never acquired NeXT? Would Jobs' impact on the tech world have been the same?

Jobs' investment in Lucasfilm's computer graphics division led to the creation of Pixar Animation Studios, resulting in tremendous success with groundbreaking films like "Toy Story."

His return to Apple in 1997 marked a turning point. His leadership and innovative vision played a pivotal role in Apple's revival and the creation of iconic products like the iMac and iPod. Jobs' involvement in developing culturally impactful products, such as the iMac, iPod, iPhone, and iPad, turned Apple around from near bankruptcy. The unplanned events, fortunate circumstances, and strokes of luck, combined with his vision and determination, reshaped the technology landscape and solidified his status as one of the most influential figures in modern history.

15. Walt Disney

Walt Disney's journey to becoming a renowned name in the entertainment industry was far from straightforward. It involved a combination of deliberate efforts, creative brilliance, and lucky breaks. Let's explore some key moments in Disney's life where chance, probability, and unforeseen events played a significant role in shaping his success.

In 1919, while working at a newspaper, Disney was unexpectedly fired by an editor who saw him as uncreative and devoid of ideas. This sudden transition from a shy and self-deprecating individual to a warm and outgoing public figure played a significant role in his public appeal and connection with audiences.

Disney's introduction to animation was a chance encounter. While working as a cartoonist, he discovered animation and was captivated by it. His partnership with Ub Iwerks, another stroke of luck, led to the creation of Oswald the Lucky Rabbit. Although Disney lost the rights to Oswald, this setback ultimately led to the creation of Mickey Mouse, an even more iconic character.

The creation of Mickey Mouse was also a result of chance. Disney needed fresh content to fill a gap in his production schedule, and the idea of a mouse character came to him unexpectedly. The unexpected success of Mickey Mouse transformed Disney's studio into a major animation powerhouse.

Disney faced significant financial challenges in the early days of his studio, struggling to make ends meet. It was during this time that he created "Snow White and the Seven Dwarfs." The film's success was uncertain, but it turned out to be a massive hit, solidifying Disney's position as a pioneer in animation.

Disney's films like "Snow White and the Seven Dwarfs," "Pinocchio," and "Fantasia" achieved critical and commercial success, benefiting from the timing and changing preferences of the audience.

Disney's foray into amusement parks was a bold move, and the success of Disneyland was influenced by the growing interest in family entertainment and leisure activities.

16. Winston Churchill

Winston Churchill, born in 1874, served as the Prime Minister of the United Kingdom from 1951 to 1955. His life was a tapestry of chance, luck, and unexpected events that shaped history. Born into the esteemed Churchill family, he enjoyed social advantages from the start, thanks to his aristocratic lineage. His connections and elite education were instrumental in laying the foundation for his future.

His nanny, Elizabeth Everest, provided crucial emotional support in his parents' absence, shaping his determination and honing his public speaking skills. Despite overcoming dyslexia, Churchill persevered and further developed his oratory skills after transferring schools in 1884. Passing the Harrow School entrance exam at the age of 13 was a fortunate break that paved the way for his prestigious education.

Although rejected twice by the Royal Military College, Sandhurst, Churchill's third attempt was successful. He thrived during his time there, despite earlier setbacks. His appointment as the First Lord of the Admiralty in 1911, during World War I, proved to be a pivotal moment that showcased his leadership and strategic thinking, thanks to an unexpected opportunity.

Surviving perilous situations like the Boer War and World War I was partly attributed to sheer luck, despite the enormous risks he took. Unexpectedly, failed investments led Churchill into the realm of politics. Despite facing five election losses, battling depression, and overcoming a speech impediment, he persisted in his pursuit.

Switching from the Conservative Party to the Liberal Party in 1908 was an unplanned change that prepared him for future roles. Churchill's appointment as the Chancellor of the Exchequer in 1924 came about due to the sudden death of David Lloyd George and his outspoken stance against appeasement, which eventually proved to be prophetic.

In 1940, he unexpectedly became the Prime Minister during the early days of World War II, earning admiration for his leadership. Winning the 1951 general election, despite losing the popular vote to the Labour Party, was another stroke of luck that allowed him to continue leading, despite not having the majority of public support.

Recognizing and responding to emerging geopolitical realities, such as the famous "Iron Curtain" speech in 1946, demonstrated Churchill's adaptability and his ability to seize unexpected opportunities.

The death of King George VI in 1952 created an unexpected situation that delayed any potential transition of power.

Surviving minor strokes and a serious stroke in 1953 enabled him to continue in office and extend his premiership. His friendship with Queen Elizabeth II and his knighthood added a personal dimension to his role, influencing his dynamics of leadership.

Becoming the Prime Minister during World War II was a critical moment where his powerful speeches inspired and motivated the people. His close relationship with President Franklin D. Roosevelt played a pivotal role in shaping the course of the war and post-war geopolitics.

Numerous chance events, interactions, and timely decisions played a role in Churchill's remarkable journey. His ability to navigate through these uncertainties left an indelible mark on history.

17. Srinivasa Ramanujan

A renowned mathematician, Srinivasa Ramanujan, was born in 1887 in Tamil Nadu, India. Despite facing poverty and lacking formal education, Ramanujan made significant contributions to number theory, infinite series, and continued fractions. His mathematical brilliance caught the attention of the esteemed mathematician G.H. Hardy at Cambridge University.

Ramanujan's upbringing in an education-oriented community played a vital role in his success. His family instilled a strong emphasis on learning and nurtured his mathematical interests from a young age. Fortunately, his extraordinary talent and dedication were discovered by Prof. G.H. Hardy, who recognized his genius and invited him to study in England. This encounter changed the course of Ramanujan's life, allowing him to share his ideas with other mathematicians and advance his career.

Another crucial factor in Ramanujan's success was his unconventional approach to problem-solving. His unique perspective on mathematics enabled him to unveil connections and patterns that had eluded other mathematicians. This unplanned and unexpected factor significantly contributed to his remarkable contributions in the field.

Ramanujan faced challenges in adapting to life in England and experienced discrimination. Additionally, his health was fragile, and he battled various ailments throughout his life. However, with Hardy's support and recognition of his brilliance, he overcame these obstacles and achieved success.

Ramanujan's story emphasizes the significance of chance, unexpected events, and luck in shaping one's success. While hard work and talent are crucial, there are always external factors beyond our control that influence our path in life. It is important to acknowledge and appreciate the role of chance in our successes, rather than attributing everything solely to personal effort or skill.

One can't help but wonder what would have happened if Ramanujan's family didn't value education or if he had never been discovered by Prof. Hardy. Would he still have made his remarkable contributions to mathematics? The answer is unknowable, but it underscores the importance of recognizing the role of chance in our lives.

18. Amitabh Bachchan

The inspiring tale of Amitabh Bachchan underscores the significance of unexpected and random factors in his life, highlighting the role of fate and luck in shaping his remarkable journey.

Amitabh initially faced rejections due to his height and deep voice, which were perceived as disadvantages in the film industry at the time. Despite these challenges, he persevered, and his breakthrough came unexpectedly with the movie "Saat Hindustani," earning him a national award. This unplanned success opened new doors for him, leading to iconic roles in films like "Anand" and "Zanjeer," marking a turning point in his career.

Life took an unforeseen turn when he met with a near-fatal accident on the sets of "Coolie." Many believed this could be the end of his career, but his resilience and quick recovery defied the odds. However, the incident left him with a lingering health condition that he continues to battle. This phase of his life exemplifies the unpredictability of fate and the challenges one must overcome.

Amitabh's career faced another downturn in his late 50s, with financial troubles and a series of unsuccessful movies. In the early 2000s, he found himself in a situation where he had lost a significant portion of his earnings and struggled to secure roles. This unexpected setback led him to approach his friend Yash Chopra for a role in "Mohabbatein," showcasing the capricious nature of success and the need to adapt to changing circumstances.

The pivotal moment in his career came with the offer to host "Kaun Banega Crorepati," a move that was initially met with skepticism by some. This unplanned transition from the silver screen to television turned out to be a game-changer. Amitabh's response, "beggars can't be choosers," reflects his willingness to embrace opportunities, even if they deviate from the expected path.

Through the highs and lows, Amitabh Bachchan's life imparts valuable lessons. His quote, "Bad luck can either destroy you or reveal the person you are," emphasizes the importance of resilience in the face of adversity.

Acknowledging mistakes and limitations, he advocates for continuous learning and improvement. Amitabh's life story encourages everyone to focus on the present, learn from the past, and persevere in the face of uncertainty, embodying the idea that success often arises from the unexpected twists of fate.

Part III.
Who Decides Your Fate?

17. The Crucial Yes

"Traffic" is a Malayalam movie released in 2011. The story unfolds on a significant day in Kochi, where the lives of various individuals become interconnected. Superstar Sidharth Shankar prepares for the release of his new movie, while Traffic Constable Sudevan returns to work after a suspension for accepting a bribe to support his niece's education. Dr. Abel celebrates his first wedding anniversary, and aspiring journalist Raihan starts his new job with an interview of Sidharth Shankar.

Tragedy strikes when Raihan and Rajeev are involved in a fatal accident at a busy traffic junction in Kochi. Raihan falls into a coma and is declared brain dead. Meanwhile, Siddharth's daughter Riya's health deteriorates, and she urgently needs a heart transplant. Raihan's heart is a potential match, but transporting it from Kochi to Palakkad proves to be a significant challenge due to poor road conditions. Unfortunately, bad weather prevents the use of helicopters.

The heart needs to travel 156 km in just two hours, a seemingly impossible task due to the poor state of the roads. Initially, the city police commissioner refuses to allow this journey due to concerns about impracticality, potential headaches, traffic problems, probable accidents, and chaos.

However, the hospital chairman persuades the police commissioner with these words: "Mr. Commissioner, saying 'no' would make today like any other day, with no significant difference in your life or mine. We would all have a peaceful day.

But if you say 'yes,' it might be a day of immense stress for all of us, maybe even for the entire state of Kerala. However, it could also be a historic day that inspires many to make positive choices." These words prompt the police commissioner to say a daring 'yes.'

For the first time in Kerala, a heart is transported through heavily congested and narrow roads, something that everyone thought was impossible. The surgery is successful, and the girl's life is saved.

The movie's message is clear: when those in positions of authority say "yes," they can inspire many to make positive choices. It encourages decision-makers to look beyond bureaucracy and red tape, giving people a chance to take the first step toward progress. By saying "yes," they become the guiding light for many and bring numerous talents to the forefront. The world has been shaped by those who dared to say "yes."

Those who faced "No"

A young man from Fort Kochi, Kerala applied to sing on All India Radio after earning diplomas like Ganabhushanam and Sangeetha Bhushanam. However, a superior denied him the opportunity, claiming his voice wasn't good. Ironically, this same young man later became the renowned singer KJ Yesudas, who won eight national awards for the best singer and is considered one of the greatest singers in India. He is addressed as Ganadandharvan, or Celestial Singer.

Similarly, despite her famous father's support and friendship with the Nehru family, Amitabh Bachchan couldn't secure a job as an announcer on All India Radio due to someone deeming her voice inadequate. Yet, the rest is history.

In mid-2009, a software engineer with twelve years of experience at Yahoo and Apple Computers faced rejection from two internet giants at the time - first Twitter, then Facebook. Unable to secure another job, he co-created an application. This person is none other than Brian Acton, who later developed WhatsApp. In 2014, Facebook acquired WhatsApp for $19 billion, making Acton's net worth $3.8 billion.

In 1919, while employed at a newspaper, he was fired by the editor who deemed him uncreative and devoid of ideas. Despite the setback, this resilient young man birthed his most successful cartoon character - Mickey Mouse. Yes, this individual is none other than entrepreneur, cartoonist, animator, voice actor, and filmmaker Walt Disney.

As these examples show, many others with stories of rejection have inspiring narratives that often go unnoticed. The message is, by saying "yes" to someone, you can offer an opportunity that transforms their life, creating an indelible legacy. So, when approached by someone seeking assistance, contemplate responding with "yes" and extending the support they require to move ahead. Saying "yes" today might just pave the path for a brighter tomorrow for someone.

The difficult first step

As mentioned earlier, climbing the first step to success is the most important and challenging task. The initial milestone is positioned much higher up and is protected by those who are already successful. To reach this first stage, you need a helping hand to start your journey. Being a part of the establishment is the first and most difficult step towards success.

There's a saying about the Canadian job market - for getting a job here, it doesn't matter what you know; it's who you know. Yes, passing this initial hurdle is the toughest part. Sadly, people often put in less effort to give a helping hand, but these same people will put in considerable effort to harm his prosperity.

18. The Auspicious Times And Omens

People often have an inherent tendency to associate the happenings in their lives with something supernatural. Countless unfounded and unscientific beliefs exist throughout the world. While eastern countries are flooded with such beliefs about supernatural forces driving their lives, the west, with a more scientific temperament, is not completely free from them.

One widely accepted factor worldwide is the importance of an auspicious time. When faced with failure, people often attribute it to "bad timing." This concept of timing is often viewed and interpreted through celestial, astrological, neurological, or similar pseudo-scientific lenses. In India, this belief is particularly prevalent, with individuals placing firm faith in the divine influence of timing.

Astrological time units like nimesha, kāṣṭhā, kalā, and ghatika are employed to determine a child's future and subsequent activities. These units resemble standard time measurements of hours, minutes, and seconds. Birth charts and horoscopes in Indian astrology are created by calculating these units, relying heavily on stars positioned many light-years away or planets like Mars, which are 225km - 401 million km away from Earth.

The Villain Moon

The idea that the moon has a significant influence on human behavior has been debated for centuries and has shaped cultural beliefs. However, scientific studies have largely disproven this claim. In this exploration, we will delve into the historical origins of lunar influence, examine scientific perspectives, and uncover enduring myths surrounding the moon's supposed impact on human life.

Ancient Beliefs and Modern Misconceptions

The phrase "It must be a full moon" dates back to the beliefs of ancient thinkers like Aristotle and Pliny the Elder, who attributed madness to the full moon. This hypothesis gave rise to the term "lunatic."

Even modern thinkers like psychiatrist Arnold Lieber explored the idea that the moon's gravitational pull, affecting the body's water content, could lead to negative behaviors. However, scientific scrutiny has dismissed these theories, highlighting the minimal influence of the moon's gravitational force compared to Earth's.

Astronomers, physicists, and psychologists have conducted extensive studies to examine the relationship between lunar phases and human behavior. A meta-analysis in 1985 examined 37 studies and found no correlation between the full moon and crises, suicides, crimes, or psychiatric issues. Numerous modern studies have echoed these findings, debunking the persistent belief in a lunar effect on behaviors such as aggression and hospital admissions.

Why does this belief persist?

Despite scientific evidence debunking lunar influence, superstitions continue to persist. One explanation lies in the concept of illusory correlation and confirmation bias. People tend to notice and remember events that align with their beliefs, reinforcing the notion of a lunar effect. Psychologist Amy Morin suggests that the expectation of unusual occurrences during a full moon may create a self-fulfilling prophecy, influencing behavior based on cultural beliefs.

Cultural and Spiritual Significance

The moon holds immense significance in various cultures and spiritual practices. Indigenous cultures honor the moon for its role in regulating tides and marking significant periods. In astrology, the moon's influence extends to emotional and intuitive aspects, shaping beliefs about individual moon signs. Mindfully aligning with the lunar cycle has become a spiritual and self-care practice, with each phase corresponding to specific actions and intentions.

Health and the Moon

Beliefs associating the moon with health have deep historical roots. From warding off lunar eclipse effects in Mesopotamia to the supposed impact on menstrual cycles, these connections persist. However, scientifically, there is limited evidence supporting a direct link between the moon and health. While ancient practices and beliefs endure, the scientific community emphasizes caution when attributing health-related phenomena to the moon.

To simplify scientifically, the moon's gravitational pull has a minimal impact on our bodies, even less than the weight of a mosquito resting on your hand. While the moon's gravity significantly affects large bodies like oceans, its influence on a 70 kg human is negligible.

When Time Truly Matters

Let's turn our focus to the concept of "time" and its significance to humans. Time has a profound and unpredictable influence on everything. It impacts every aspect of our lives. Let's take a closer look at it. Consider the moment of conception, when a sperm fertilizes an egg, leading to the formation of a zygote. This specific timing can make a significant difference in one's life.

The quality of eggs and sperm can decline with age. Female fertility tends to decrease, with a more pronounced decline after the age of 35. For women, the quality of eggs can be influenced by the menstrual cycle, with the best-quality eggs typically released during ovulation, which occurs around the middle of the cycle. In men, various lifestyle factors such as diet, exercise, and overall health can influence sperm quality. Unlike women, men continuously produce sperm, but certain factors like illness, medication, or lifestyle choices can temporarily affect its quality.

At the moment of conception, genetic information from both parents combines, determining inherited traits such as physical characteristics, susceptibility to diseases, and aspects of personality. These genetic factors play a crucial role in shaping an individual's life right from the start.

During pregnancy, various external factors that are beyond the mother's control can significantly influence the baby's development. Exposure to toxins, radiation, allergens, or pollutants poses potential risks to the developing fetus. These environmental elements can adversely affect the baby's growth and may contribute to developmental issues.

Furthermore, the mother's emotional and mental well-being during pregnancy plays a crucial role in shaping the baby's early brain development and emotional health. Stress, anxiety, and depression experienced by the mother can have profound effects on the developing fetus, impacting neural connections and emotional regulation.

The conditions and experiences during the prenatal period extend beyond the immediate pregnancy. They can have enduring effects on the individual's physical and mental health throughout their life. The prenatal environment can influence cognitive abilities, emotional resilience, and even the susceptibility to certain diseases in later stages of life.

It is essential to understand that these influences are based on biological and environmental factors, rather than any notion of auspicious or inauspicious timing.

The Significance of Time

Let's closely examine the importance of time

Scene 1: A man seeks to unveil his destiny from a fortune teller who predicts imminent success and wishes him good luck. Departing from the fortune teller's office at 10:32 in the morning, he steps onto the road at 10:32 and 10 seconds. Suddenly, a speeding vehicle screeches and collides with him, knocking him down.

Scene 2: Similarly, as he leaves the fortune teller's place at 10:32, he notices his phone ringing, retrieves it from his pocket, and, after realizing it's unnecessary, ends the call and puts the phone back in his pocket. This process wastes 15 seconds. He reaches the road at 10:32 and 25 seconds. Fortunately, the first vehicle had passed 15 seconds earlier, allowing him to avoid the accident this time.

Scene 3: Once again, he exits the fortune teller's room at 10:30 and 10 seconds. As in the previous scene, he receives a call. Choosing not to answer, another 15 seconds pass by. He arrives at the road at 10:32 and 25 seconds, but unfortunately, the first vehicle arrives 10 seconds late, coinciding exactly with the time the man steps onto the road, resulting in a fatal accident.

In reality, randomness plays a crucial role in determining an individual's success or failure in life. The people we encounter, our study companions, the friendships we form, and the circumstances these relationships lead to—all greatly influence our path to success. Even the smallest decisions we make can drastically alter our lives, with numerous factors coming into play when making these choices. The same person may make different decisions at night compared to during the day due to factors such as hunger, illness, or weather.

Those immersed in the fortune-telling and cold reading business often rely on judgmental biases and perceptual biases to promote their ideas. It is crucial to critically analyze the examples and concepts presented in these books and understand that the lives of remarkable individuals are shaped by countless random events, not all of which are pleasant. As mentioned earlier, many of these experiences can be overwhelming, and success encompasses all the events that occur in life, whether they are beneficial or challenging.

Therefore, it is essential to recognize that achievements in a person's life may not always stem from happy experiences. They can involve hardships such as war, lack of freedom, disease, poverty, or wealth. Success is a multifaceted outcome influenced by a myriad of unpredictable factors and experiences.

Great men time created

The best example to illustrate this point is Mahatma Gandhi. He was born during a time of oppression and lack of freedom. If Gandhi were born in the present day, he would have encountered different challenges and opportunities.

Similarly, let's consider Michael Jackson or Elvis Presley, the greatest singers. If they were born in 2000, they would have faced a different musical landscape and perhaps would have been just ordinary YouTubers.

The same could be said for Bill Gates, Nelson Mandela, Charlie Chaplin, Winston Churchill, Abraham Lincoln, and even the incredibly talented Bruce Lee. Their destinies would have been altered if they were born in the last thirty years. Time plays a pivotal role in shaping the fate of individuals, regardless of their exceptional gifts. This perspective holds true for all great individuals throughout history.

There was widespread concern within the intellectual community when Dolly, the cloned sheep, made headlines in the scientific world. People pondered the potential consequences if humans could be cloned, raising fears of secret figures emerging, akin to Hitler or Idi Amin. However, even if an individual resembling Hitler were to be created, the present world would not provide the conditions for them to replicate their actions. Consequently, they would remain ordinary individuals, bearing resemblance to historical figures but unable to re-enact their deeds due to the transformed global landscape.

So, in reality success is not solely determined by an individual's talents or abilities but is also influenced by the environment in which they exist. It is crucial to acknowledge that success can be shaped by various factors, including random events and encounters. Furthermore, the world plays a significant role in shaping our destiny.

19. How Easily Can You Be Deceived?

When Kerala's most prominent IPS and IAS officers flocked to buy and see the official stamp document of the Mysore palace, the throne of Tipu Sultan, and the objects used by religious figures like Moses, Jesus Christ, and Lord Krishna, our pride was humbled. However, before you begin to scorn the rest of those who were deceived by this con man, consider one thing: you too may be fooled just as easily like anyone else.

Monson Mavunkal, a self-proclaimed antique dealer, has been arrested by the Crime Branch Police following complaints from six individuals accusing him of cheating and forgery. The charges involve him allegedly pocketing Rs.10 crore from these individuals over a period starting from 2017.

Monson has described himself as a world peace promoter, philanthropist, educationist, and motivational speaker on his website, but is currently facing police investigation for alleged fraudulent activities.

Among his other claims, Monson stated that he possessed two of the 30 coins received by Judas for betraying Jesus, a piece of clothing worn by Jesus, the chalice used by Prophet Mohammed, and the throne of Tipu Sultan, as well as many other mythological items.

Following Monson's arrest, media reports about his private museum in Kochi have gone viral on social media, with attention drawn to his alleged collection of paintings by Leonardo da Vinci and Raja Ravi Varma, a copy of the

Bhagavad Gita belonging to Chhatrapati Shivaji, relics from the Bible's Old Testament, the hand fan of Sree Narayana Guru, the throne of the Travancore king, the first-ever gramophone, the first printed Bible in the world, and the Quran used by Saddam Hussain, among various other items. These claims will now be inspected by the police.

Is this a rarest of rare case? No, this kind of cheating is happening all over the world regularly. Let us look at another interesting example:

An Italian artist has successfully auctioned an 'invisible sculpture' for $18,300. Salvatore Garao, the artist behind it, described the artwork as "literally nothing" and believes it prompts viewers to engage their imagination.

According to Garou, the sculpture titled Lo Sono (which translates to "I") derives its form from its emptiness.

He explained that a vacuum may seem devoid of substance, but it is actually filled with energy. In light of the Heisenberg uncertainty principle, even when emptied, it retains energy, which then condenses into particles – including ourselves. The "spectacle" fetched a price far higher than its original value, and the fortunate buyer received a certificate of authenticity and a set of instructions for the sculpture.

Notably, this isn't Garao's first venture into the realm of invisible art. He previously exhibited another invisible sculpture called Contemplation of the Buddha in Milan's Piazza della Scala.

The World of Scams

Some of the most notorious scams include Nigerian lottery schemes. It's challenging to determine the exact number of victims each year, as many people who fall prey to these scams do not report their losses. However, it is estimated that billions of dollars are lost annually due to this fraudulent activity. What is their modus operandi?

To begin with, these scammers send approximately a million emails daily, hoping that at least a thousand people will respond and succeed in deceiving at least a few.

The scam is deceptively simple. Victims receive an email claiming they have won a foreign lottery worth millions of rupees, or they are approached by a wealthy individual seeking assistance in transferring money out of their country. In exchange for their help, the victims are promised a substantial sum of money. The catch is that the victims must first send a small amount of money to the scammer. In reality, many more people fall victim to this scam than expected by the fraudsters.

This Nigerian fraud scheme is one of the oldest in the world and continues to thrive today, exploiting people's greed and desire for quick and easy money, making it a persistent and ongoing problem.

The next most common area of concern is investment scams, which can deceive even the most confident and educated individuals. Countless frauds have been committed in our country, ranging from multi-level marketing schemes to more sophisticated forms, stealing crores of rupees from unsuspecting people.

Fortune tellers and psychics also deceive millions of people by claiming to predict the future. They use visual cues, such as age, clothes, and body language, to make high-level, off-the-cuff statements. This technique is known as cold reading in English, and while some of their predictions may come true, it's mostly a form of deception. We will examine this in detail in the coming chapters.

Fake news and misinformation have become rampant with the rise of social media. Every day, a tsunami of false information floods our feeds, easily fooling even the most educated individuals. This misinformation can lead to the formation of false opinions or decisions based on incorrect information.

To avoid falling victim to these scams, it's essential to be aware of their existence and be cautious when encountering unsolicited offers or requests for personal information. Never send money to someone you don't know, and be wary of any opportunity that seems too good to be true. Additionally, fact-check information before sharing it on social media to prevent the spread of misinformation. By being informed and vigilant, we can protect ourselves from the world of scams.

The Third Person Effect: Someone, Somewhere Will Be Misled

You may have heard people saying, "I personally believe everything after thoroughly analyzing it deeply, taking into account my experiences and knowledge before accepting it." However, some people readily believe even the biggest lies spread around them. I can quickly discern politicians' lies, but some individuals seem to believe anything they hear, especially when it comes through a microphone or printed or in a WhatsApp video. No one can deceive me so easily.

In truth, each person thinks and believes in a similar manner. We often undervalue others' arguments if they differ from our beliefs, considering them misguided and easily deceived. Interestingly, this is also how each person judges themselves.

Now, let's imagine you have to listen to dangerous messages, misleading advertisements, or deceptive speeches. You might think you are not affected by them, but in reality, with the prevalence of electronic media, we are bombarded with hundreds of such misleading messages every second, and they can influence us directly or indirectly.

Affinity Bias

We may have heard stories of people who performed poorly in technical interviews but still got the job because they shared the same interests or played the same games as the manager. Human resource managers believe they are excellent judges of character, only to be disappointed when the person they hired leaves the company within a month. Often, we tend to choose candidates who align with our likes, dislikes, living conditions, and beliefs.

As a manager, you might have encountered instances where exceptionally talented individuals were rejected solely because the chemistry didn't feel right.

Unconscious Perceptual Bias and Affinity Bias are interconnected. Affinity Bias is an unconscious process driven by our brain's efforts to minimize energy expenditure. With approximately eleven million pieces of information entering our brains every moment, we resort to shortcuts to make decisions. These are called heuristics. When meeting new people, we unconsciously judge them based on factors like gender, ethnicity, appearance, color, and religion, often before we're consciously aware of it. With the heuristics or shortcuts, we easily jump into conclusive judgments.

Managers may unintentionally choose individuals who fit into a predetermined cultural framework they believe to be correct. This approach can discourage many intelligent candidates and create a company culture with homogenous mindsets, limiting the potential for new and diverse ideas to flourish. Embracing diversity can lead to remarkable results and innovation

Part IV.
The Para Spaces

20. Negative Energy - Belief And Business

The phenomena of negative energy and negative vibrations have recently gained attention and are now widely discussed everywhere. Conversations about places with negative energy, techniques for clearing negative energy from a room, factors that generate negative energy, and sources emitting negative vibrations are encountered frequently. YouTube is filled with methods for expelling negative energy, and mainstream media regularly publishes articles on this topic.

However, if you ask these self-help spiritual gurus about what exactly is termed negative energy, you will find that they all have different opinions, and no two answers are the same. Each person holds their own unique perspective on what negative energy truly means, how to get rid of it, and how to deal with it.

Whatever definition each one assigns to negative vibrations, the ways they advise to avoid them are innumerable. It's like opening Pandora's box of expertise, where some rely on specific stones, while others turn to divine objects, prayers, mantras, or even lime and green tea. There is no consensus on the methods, as each approach is shaped by individual emotions, whims, and fantasies.

Moreover, the concept of negative energy has an intriguing connection to superstitions and pseudo-scientific beliefs. It seamlessly intertwines with various irrational convictions and deceptive doctrines, showcasing its ability to coexist harmoniously within this realm.

The question remains: What is negative energy? Despite the differing opinions and numerous methods for dealing with it, one thing is certain—the power of negative energy and its effects on our lives are widely accepted by a major chunk of the population.

What is Negative Energy?

Negative energy is a concept used in physics to explain certain characteristics of gravitational fields and quantum field effects. The term "negative energy" is also applied in various other scientific fields. For example, we know that the freezing point of water is 0 degrees Celsius. When the temperature drops below this point, we refer to it as negative temperatures or minus degrees Celsius. In thermodynamics, the concept of negative energy exists.

Let's consider a flashlight battery. If you were to touch the negative pole of the battery, would negative energy transfer to you? Similarly, if you touch the positive pole, would positive energy transmit to you? As you may know, none of these scenarios actually happen. This is because the use of the terms "energy" and "negative energy" in physics has no connection to the deceptive doctrines found in pseudosciences.

It is noteworthy that discussions about eliminating or dissipating negative energy continue to attract significant attention and viewership. However, the scientific understanding clearly states that no such thing as negative energy really exists. Unfortunately, there are only a limited number of YouTube videos available that effectively debunk this misconception.

But we surely feel negative energy. Why?

When we interact with specific individuals, we sometimes feel upset without any reason. Let's explore the reasons behind this. As we encounter certain people, we might notice aspects that don't resonate positively with us. Factors such as their background, social status, religion, culture, appearance, clothing, language, and more might not align with our preferences. Furthermore, their body language can contribute to our mindset. This interaction can evoke emotions like happiness, fear, envy, insecurity, or a sense of protection within our own mental landscape.

Interestingly, our brains struggle to differentiate between actual threats and perceived ones. Thus, our brain might interpret someone's outward demeanor as a threat. Some label this as negative energy. However, it's important to note that there's no true negative energy emanating from another person that affects you.

The same situation can be experienced differently by various individuals. For instance, consider complimenting an elderly woman from an Indian village. You say, "Aunty, you look really nice today." Despite your positive intention, she might feel uneasy and insecure. This is because she believes that receiving compliments on her appearance might bring harm, and she fears her health could deteriorate.

In contrast, if you offer the same compliment to an American woman, saying, "Hey Susan, you look beautiful today, and your choice of clothing is fantastic," she would likely feel joyful upon hearing this. Such affirmations boost her self-confidence and contribute to her mental well-being. This positivity ripples through her actions, leading to an overall positive impact on her mental state.

In reality, what we term as negative energy originates from within your mind. This implies that your mental attitude toward a situation determines whether you perceive it positively or negatively. You then label it as negative or positive energy. Feelings of happiness, sadness, or excitement arise due to the activity of neurotransmitters in the human brain.

For instance, seeing an appealing piece of clothing evokes diverse emotions in different people. The same color can elicit happiness in one person and discomfort or fear in another.

In simpler terms, the shifts in neurotransmitters in your brain are what we call negative or positive energy. A statement that brings happiness to one person could evoke sadness in someone else. Likewise, a song or a specific place can bring immense joy to some while causing restlessness and fear in others.

To conclude, changes in neurotransmitters in your brain lead to the variations in what you perceive as negative or positive energy. In India, major media outlets discuss this topic in-depth weekly, offering various techniques to counteract negative energy. It's empirically proven that our mental interpretations of situations are interpreted as negative or positive energy.

However, this isn't limited to Indian media. I'd like to share an unfortunate observation. Even reputable worldwide medical information sources like WebMD delve into negative energy. They don't explicitly state that it's entirely a product of the mind. Their explanation can be misleading, giving the impression that something called negative energy really exists. When you encounter specific places, you might feel uneasy for no obvious reason. Regular inhabitants of those places often experience negative energy and various unusual phenomena. Even rationalists or scientific advocates sometimes feel this. Why does this occur? Numerous scientific and psychological explanations exist beyond mere feelings. Allow me to illustrate this point with an experience from my professional life.

The Out of Body Experience of a girl

Revathi, a nursing student, was brought to me by her brother. She had been feeling distressed for a while. Her experience was peculiar. After moving into her new hostel room, she started having vivid dreams and woke up feeling terrified. In her dreams, she felt trapped in a room, while her body remained in bed. This phenomenon only occurred in this specific room. Other people who stayed in the room also reported strange experiences.

Revathi didn't believe in ghosts, but these occurrences mentally distressed her. She didn't face such issues in other places or rooms. The room had a history of a student committing suicide, and people believed that powerful negative energy lingered there. Various rituals and religious ceremonies were performed to eradicate the negativity, but they were ineffective.

After further conversation, I realized that Revathi's problems weren't just her imagination or personal perceptions. The room was plagued by hypoxia.

Hypoxia

Hypoxia is a condition that occurs when body tissues do not receive enough oxygen for their essential functions. When the blood lacks sufficient oxygen, it leads to hypoxemia, which is low oxygen in the tissues, resulting in hypoxia. "Hypoxia" refers to two distinct issues, both of which pose serious health risks, especially when oxygen levels drop below a critical point.

Hypoxia manifests with various symptoms. Common signs of mild hypoxia include changes in skin color, confusion, coughing, increased heart rate, rapid breathing, shortness of breath, decreased heart rate, sweating, and wheezing. The effects of hypoxia can vary depending on its severity and duration. In severe cases, individuals may experience hallucinations, impaired judgment, and even loss of consciousness. Immediate medical attention is necessary to restore oxygen levels and prevent complications in cases of severe hypoxia.

Elevated levels of carbon dioxide in the bloodstream can cause disturbances and trigger mental unease. Phenomena such as seeing apparitions, sensing bright lights, or encountering celestial beings or departed souls are rooted in physiological changes rather than metaphysical influences. It is important to emphasize that these disturbances arise from physiological factors, not external metaphysical influences.

Let's consider Revathi's living space as an example. Her room lacks proper air circulation due to the release of contaminated air from the hospital's incinerator. Inhaling this polluted air can cause respiratory irritation and disrupt sleep patterns. This issue is not related to negative energy but rather results from airborne impurities.

In Revathi's case, her situation improved when she moved to a room with better air circulation.

The concept of negative energy or vibrations lacks scientific evidence to support its existence. It is often exploited by pseudoscientific practitioners who prey on people's fear of the unknown. These practitioners may claim to remove negative energy, but there is no scientific proof to substantiate their claims.

Believing in negative energy can be harmful and can lead to psychological distress such as anxiety and depression. Such unfounded beliefs can have damaging effects.

It is crucial to approach claims about negative energy with skepticism. Instead, rely on evidence-based practices and seek assistance from qualified mental health professionals when facing emotional challenges. Embracing a rational perspective promotes a healthier mindset and reduces unnecessary stress.

Human Aura

Kirlian photography, a technique named after Semyon Davidovich Kirlian, has been known to physicists and electrical engineers for a long time. It captures the occurrence of an electric spark seemingly generating its own image on a photographic emulsion. This type of photography does not require a traditional camera. The scientific community has understood and explained this phenomenon since the early days of photography.

Kirlian photographs display luminous energy discharges around objects, resembling a halo or aura. However, it is important to recognize that these images are not produced using a specific camera designed for capturing auras or human energy fields. Instead, Kirlian photos are created using electrified photographic plates, which create a captivating visual effect but do not conclusively prove the existence of auras or human energy fields.

Unfortunately, some individuals, lacking a thorough understanding of scientific principles, have associated Kirlian photography with supernatural concepts like the "aura" or "human energy field." These ideas gained popularity through figures like Madame Helena P. Blavatsky, a prominent occultist. The notion of the human aura became prominent within New Age and spiritual circles, proposing that all living beings possess a radiant energy field surrounding their bodies, offering insights into their physical, emotional, and spiritual states.

However, science has repeatedly debunked this concept throughout history. No scientific instrument has successfully detected or measured the presumed aura. Despite being categorized as a pseudoscientific belief by the scientific community, millions of people still hold onto the belief in a supernatural aura.

Encounters with individuals who claim to perceive auras are subjective and often influenced by psychological predispositions such as confirmation bias or the placebo effect. Most of these claims could be delusions or simply outright lies.

The Extra sensory World

Is extra-sensory perception (ESP) considered scientific? It is a common tendency for humans to attribute supernatural explanations to things that cannot be explained through common sense. Despite the revolutionary accessibility of information technology, where anyone with basic education can easily research the scientific nature of various phenomena on their smartphones, people still prefer to believe in the supernatural. We tend to believe what aligns with our desires.

Now, let's delve into the key terms related to psychic powers and ESP:

Intuition: It involves having foreknowledge or understanding something without relying on physical evidence, reasoning, or information. It is the ability to grasp hidden aspects, such as predicting the outcome of an election.

Telepathy: Telepathy allows the transmission of messages to another person's mind without the need for any communication device or medium. Some individuals claim to possess the ability to read the thoughts of others.

Psychometry: Psychometry is a technique where one predicts the future or gains insights by touching certain objects and sensing the energy associated with them.

Clairvoyance: It refers to the ability to see distant events or occurrences with divine insight, even if they are happening far away.
Precognition: Precognition involves the ability to predict future events and is one of the most popular subjects within the realm of psychic abilities.
Retrocognition: This ability entails revealing information about one's past life, including their identity and place of residence. Although relatively less popular, it is overshadowed by people's inclination towards future predictions.

The fascination with knowing the future has contributed to the popularity of various methods associated with future forecasting, clairvoyance, and supernatural powers. While magicians like Harry Houdini and David Copperfield are renowned for their tricks, some individuals with limited knowledge of magic claim to possess divine abilities. Surprisingly, these individuals often earn significantly more money than highly skilled magicians.

In a 2005 survey conducted in the United States, 41 percent of respondents expressed belief in supernatural powers. Even 73 percent of American psychology graduate students admitted to believing in psychic abilities.

The Stargate Project

One notable project linked to psychic phenomena is the Stargate project, which was funded by the US government from 1972 to 1995. With a budget of $20 million, the project aimed to explore the potential use of individuals with spiritual siddhis (supernatural powers) to gather intelligence that conventional methods couldn't obtain. The Stargate Project, though now declassified, was a genuine government program that focused on investigating psychic phenomena, specifically remote viewing.

Remote viewing involves individuals attempting to gather information about distant or unseen targets, surpassing the limits of normal human perception. The Stargate Project employed individuals with psychic abilities, including remote viewers, and conducted experiments to evaluate the validity and reliability of their claims. However, the project faced widespread criticism from the scientific community due to the lack of empirical support and methodological issues.

In 1995, the Stargate Project was declassified, and its documents were made public. While some find the project intriguing, others dismiss it as pseudoscience. The perception of the Stargate Project as "ridiculous" often depends on individual beliefs, skepticism towards paranormal phenomena, and opinions on the credibility of government-funded initiatives.

The truth behind paranormal phenomena

Beliefs that are deeply ingrained in our minds from an early age tend to be resistant to change through education alone. Many of these beliefs are rooted in the powerful emotion of fear, and the mainstream media often plays a significant role in perpetuating superstitions.

Despite the advancements in science and technology, numerous TV shows in the United States have subtly delved into these hidden truths. Many movies have been released to celebrate the idea that we possess immense untapped power within ourselves.

A multitude of self-help books emphasize the notion that each individual harbors dormant supernatural potential. Training programs such as Transcendental Meditation, Mid Brain Activation, Kundalini Awakening, and Will Power Training aim to unlock this dormant power.

The belief that humans are distinct from other animals, possessing a soul, the potential for life after death, and the ability to achieve miraculous feats often leads people to embrace these supernatural powers.

In a 1987 study, 67 percent of respondents claimed to have experienced some form of psychic phenomenon. For instance, consider when you dream of a long-lost friend whom you haven't seen in years, and the following morning that friend unexpectedly calls you. It can be challenging to attribute this event purely to chance, as our memory tends to reinforce experiences that align with our desires and beliefs. However, such occurrences can be understood as random events governed by the phenomenon known as the "Law of Truly Large Numbers."

The "Law of Truly Large Numbers" suggests that in a sufficiently large sample size, even highly improbable events are likely to occur. This concept, often associated with statistics and probability theory, manifests in various ways in real life, leading to surprising coincidences. One classic example is the Birthday Paradox, which states that in a group of just 23 people, there is a higher than even chance that two people share the same birthday. While initially counterintuitive, considering all possible pairs within the group increases the probability.

Ouija Boards and Communicating with Spirits

Throughout history, cultures have engaged in practices to communicate with spirits and predict the future or delve into the past. One popular method for this is the Ouija board.

The Ouija board consists of a flat surface with letters and numbers, and participants use a coin or pointer to spell out messages. When people believe that spirits are present, they attribute the movement of the coin to the spirits answering their questions.

The use of Ouija boards dates back as early as the 3rd century (371 AD). In the past, a priest would use a vessel with a ring attached by a thread to spell out messages for the audience. The ring would appear to move on its own in response to questions, and the information was derived from the pattern of movement.

From a scientific perspective, the phenomenon of Ouija boards and spirit communication is generally attributed to the ideomotor effect and psychological factors rather than supernatural forces. Here's a breakdown of the scientific explanations:

Ideomotor Effect: This psychological phenomenon explains that individuals make unconscious and involuntary movements in response to their thoughts or expectations. When using a Ouija board, participants may unknowingly move the pointer based on their expectations or desires, creating the illusion of spirit communication.

Expectation and Suggestion: The power of suggestion and participants' expectations play a significant role. If individuals believe they can communicate with spirits through the Ouija board, they may unintentionally influence the movement of the pointer. This shared belief can create a collective experience that reinforces the idea of spirit communication.

Unconscious Movements: Participants may not be consciously aware of their movements during a Ouija board session. Subtle muscle contractions and shifts can guide the pointer across the board. Some participants may genuinely believe that external forces are at play, even though they are unconsciously moving the pointer.

Subconscious Mind: The subconscious mind can influence behavior, and the use of the Ouija board may bring forth repressed desires, fears, or thoughts, creating a perception of external communication with spirits.

Cognitive Bias: Cognitive biases, like confirmation bias, contribute to the belief in spirit communication. People tend to focus on information that confirms their belief in the supernatural while disregarding contradictory evidence. This bias reinforces the perception of a connection with spirits.

Group Dynamics: Ouija board sessions often involve multiple participants, and group dynamics, social cues, and peer pressure can influence individual behavior. Participants may unconsciously conform to the group's expectations, leading to a shared illusion of spirit communication.

In regions like America and Europe, various forms of psychic and paranormal phenomena were prevalent, with practices like "radiesthesia" or the use of divining rods causing movements. Medical radiesthesia and radionics also gained popularity in these areas. Naturopaths in the United States still use radiesthesia today.

21. The Psychology Of Cold Reading

Focus on the zodiac sign associated with your birthdate for the given week. These horoscopes often contain statements that may apply to various readers, regardless of their signs, gender, age, or location. For example, the predictions will flow like this:

There is a possibility of you visiting a special temple with your family this week. Your workload could increase as colleagues take holidays. You'll face the upcoming exam with confidence. Be cautious of a higher risk of stomach issues due to possible food poisoning. Special prayers will be offered for your spouse's foreign job. Parents might have concerns about their teenage children.

Mars might bring anger and unchecked desires this month, leading to problems. Ego conflicts and disagreements could arise due to family obligations. Approach your spouse or love interest with grace. Marriage could face difficulties due to aggressive responses. Respect and humility are important in treating your partner. Last-minute plans to visit in-laws might occur, with potential financial benefits. New job opportunities and workplace recognition are on the horizon. Success comes from acquiring new professional skills.

Mars and the Moon advise avoiding office politics and criticizing others' mistakes. It is important to recognize that these generalized statements can resonate with many individuals to some extent, as they address common experiences and emotions.

The Process of cold reading

Let's delve into the process involved in the cold reading technique used by fortune tellers. When individuals consult a fortune teller, they usually have specific concerns or issues they want to address. These can include various aspects of life such as relationships, career, and health. People seek out fortune tellers in the hope of gaining insights, advice, and remedies that can help ease their worries or provide clarity for their path forward.

The interaction with a fortune teller begins with anticipation and curiosity. As the fortune teller closes their eyes and enters a meditative state, an atmosphere of reverence and expectation is created. Skillfully, the fortune teller gathers basic information from you, such as your age, occupation, and facial expressions, all while you remain unaware of this extraction process. Using this information, along with pre-prepared statements that can apply to many people, the fortune teller begins to utter seemingly meaningful but often vague statements. These predictions are designed to fit a broad range of individuals facing similar circumstances. During this process, the fortune teller may modify their statements based on your reactions or subtly add or remove statements to make their work easier.

The Basics of Cold Reading

Cold reading is a psychological technique that allows practitioners to elicit information from a subject through observation, deduction, and subtle cues. It is not based on paranormal abilities but rather relies on the keen perception and communication skills of the reader.

Observation

Cold readers are adept at observing and interpreting physical cues, such as body language, clothing, and accessories. These visual clues offer valuable information about a person's lifestyle, occupation, or interests.

Generalized Statements

Cold readers often begin with broad and vague statements that could apply to a wide range of individuals. These generalizations create a sense of universality, making it more likely for the subject to connect with the reading.

Feedback Loop

Skilled cold readers pay close attention to the subject's responses, adjusting their approach based on the reactions received. This creates a feedback loop where the subject unknowingly provides cues that guide the direction of the reading.

The is called Barnum Effect, also known as the Forer Effect

This refers to the tendency to perceive general statements as accurate descriptions of oneself. This psychological phenomenon was first discovered by psychologist Bertram R. Forer.

Consider the following sentences about your personality:

- You desire to be loved and respected by others.
- You consciously hide some flaws in your character from the outside world.

- You often feel that you haven't reached your full potential.
- There are moments when you believe your abilities are not fully appreciated.
- Despite your disciplined mindset, occasional impatience arises.
- At times you may have moments of uncertainty.
- Some of your past decisions seem misguided.
- The influence others have had on your life now feels burdensome.
- You are an independent thinker who questions accepted norms.
- While friendly, you sometimes display introverted tendencies.
- Certain decisions may feel unreal to you.

As you read these sentences, you likely felt a personal connection. This passage was taken from a weekly magazine. In 1948, Dr. Forer gave this description to college students and asked them to rate how well the traits aligned with their own personalities on a scale from zero to five.

A score of zero indicates no alignment with the traits, while a score of five indicates complete alignment. This experiment has been reproduced over a thousand times by psychologists from different universities. The average score remains at 4.2 out of five, suggesting that 84 percent of participants perceive these traits as characteristic of themselves.

This effect extends to various professions and industries. Companies like Netflix, Amazon, and Facebook create the illusion of personalized recommendations and tailored content for each user. They skillfully employ the Barnum effect, providing users with a sense of personalization while often offering recommendations preferred by the majority.

This effect has significant implications and is present in various contexts. People often fall prey to this illusion, feeling a connection to vague descriptions that seem to capture their personalities. This tendency is not limited to psychology; it permeates many aspects of life, shaping perceptions and decisions.

The Pollyanna Principle

The theory of the Pollyanna Principle, also known as positivity bias, suggests that individuals have a tendency to remember positive events more accurately than negative ones. It makes sense, doesn't it? Why would anyone willingly choose to remember unhappy or uncomfortable events? Naturally, we gravitate towards cherishing joyful memories. This inclination also applies to the Barnum effect, where we are more likely to embrace statements that align with our desired self-perception.

Shotgun Trick

Some fortune tellers employ the "shotgun trick" by bombarding clients with a never-ending series of unrelated questions. They adapt their verses or inquiries based on the responses they receive, tailoring their approach to fit the situation. They use various jargon and sophisticated language to give themselves flexibility in interpreting the responses to support their narrative. As a result, some questions may seem to align with the individual's circumstances, while others remain ambiguous. The believer then fills in these gaps, making the process more relatable and accessible.

Rainbow Trick

The Rainbow Trick involves repeating sentences with slight variations. For example: "You are generally friendly towards everyone, although you sometimes struggle with managing anger. While you enjoy extensive travel, there are moments when you long for pure relaxation. "The listener then personalizes the parts that resonate with their own experiences.

Open-Ended Questions

These questions are open in nature and do not have a predetermined correct answer. For instance:

Fortune teller: "Was the relative who deceived you older than fifty?"

Party: "Yes, he was fifty-five years old."

Fortune teller: "That's what I sensed."

In a different scenario:

Party: "Oh, he is only thirty years old."

Fortune teller: "Ah, that's what I perceived. He's still quite young."

The open-ended nature of these questions allows for various responses, adding intrigue and adaptability to the conversation.

Fortune teller: "In your youth, you experienced a water-related accident."

Party: "No, such an incident never happened!"
Even if the fortune teller's prediction is incorrect, they continue with their verbal gymnastics. Their responses could take the form of: "Perhaps you don't remember this incident, or it's possible that your mother avoided a water-related mishap during her pregnancy. Alternatively, you might have encountered situations like consuming contaminated water or coming into contact with harmful substances."
If these possibilities don't resonate, another explanation arises: Divine forces could be trying to convey something different or imply an alternative aspect.

Hot Reading

In some instances, cold readers may employ hot reading, where they gather information about a subject beforehand through covert means. This can include online research, social media profiling, or even information obtained from accomplices.

Time-Related Statements:

Predictions about future events or revelations about past experiences are common in cold reading. However, these statements are often ambiguous and open to interpretation, allowing the reader to claim success regardless of the outcome.

Examples of a typical cold reading process:

If you are a young unmarried person, the fortune teller may say: At times, you may feel worried that marriage is out of reach for you, especially as you reach a certain age. Doubts may arise about fulfilling your destiny in marriage, and past joys may start to feel like distant memories.

For those who are already married, the following concerns may resonate: You may struggle to find comfort and satisfaction within your marriage. It might seem like your partner's affection and interest have diminished compared to earlier days. Job stress and family responsibilities can weigh heavily on your shoulders. You might also experience difficulties with memory and sleep disturbances. Furthermore, sexual issues and abdominal problems may occur frequently.

Other challenges can include disturbances caused by minor household pests, conflicts arising from the spouse's relatives and financial irresponsibility, worries about children's education, disobedience, and well-being, as well as anxieties surrounding their romantic relationships.

All of these issues are common and can significantly disrupt one's peace of mind. Additionally, workplace dilemmas with bosses and colleagues, complexities involving daughter-in-law, mother-in-law, neighbors, and numerous other predicaments can seemingly affect anyone. However, when the fortune teller mentions these pre-prepared problems, everyone believes that the seer is accurately pinpointing their specific issue.

Mastering this profession requires training, keen observation, a deep understanding of human behavior, and knowledge about current events. Interestingly, despite the generalized nature of the guidance, each individual feels as if it were uniquely tailored for them.

While cold reading may appear as a supernatural or paranormal phenomenon, it is, in reality, a well-honed skill grounded in psychology and observation. Understanding the mechanics behind cold reading empowers individuals to approach psychic or intuitive readings with a critical eye, recognizing the artistry at play and separating fact from fiction.

Handwriting and Traits (Graphology)

Graphology is the practice of analyzing handwriting to gain insights into a person's character traits. By examining factors like line spacing, word size, and other handwriting aspects, valuable information about one's personality can be revealed. Handwriting, like fingerprints, is unique to each individual, making it an intriguing subject for analysis.

However, graphology is considered a pseudoscience, similar to horoscopes, palmistry, astrology, and other forms of future prediction personality analyses. In the past, the Association of Handwriting Readers in Chicago, USA, boasted a million members and held significant influence. Some members even held official positions, such as analyzing the handwriting of teachers in a government school in Vancouver, Canada, to uncover their character traits.

Certain countries, like Israel and some in Eastern Europe, as well as major corporations, have sought the services of handwriting experts for various purposes. However, the interpretations of handwriting analysts regarding letter meanings, slant, and inclination vary greatly and lack scientific foundation. Some even promote graphotherapy, a pseudo-psychological treatment that suggests improving one's handwriting can alter personality traits and flaws. Despite this, graphology remains relatively unpopular in our country.

The Texas Sharpshooter Fallacy

The Texas Sharpshooter fallacy is a logical fallacy that occurs when individuals selectively focus on specific information while ignoring other relevant data, leading to the perception of patterns or connections that don't actually exist. This bias is a part of confirmation bias, where people seek, interpret, and remember information that supports their existing beliefs, often disregarding alternative possibilities.

The term comes from the analogy of a sharpshooter who shoots randomly and then draws a target around the cluster of bullet holes, falsely presenting themselves as a skilled marksman. Essentially, the Texas Sharpshooter fallacy highlights the tendency to amplify similarities while dismissing differences, which can result in drawing incorrect conclusions from perceived patterns that lack substance.

This fallacy often occurs when attempting to establish connections between seemingly unrelated events or information, interpreting coincidences as evidence of a specific pattern or order. Fortune tellers commonly use this line of reasoning, as seen in how some individuals interpret the prophecies of Nostradamus. After an event has occurred, these interpreters may selectively extract isolated verses from Nostradamus' work and claim that he predicted the event, disregarding inconsistencies or lack of supporting evidence in their analysis. This fallacy reinforces confirmation bias, where individuals focus on information that aligns with their preconceived notions while disregarding contradictory information.

For example, Nostradamus' prophecies mention a German warrior named "Hester," with verses like "Hungry wild beasts cross rivers. More people will be against Hyster in the war. It will put many great people in an iron pit. The son of Germany will obey no law." While some interpret this as a direct reference to Hitler, it's important to note that Nostradamus wrote numerous similar accounts of fighters from German origins. Furthermore, "Hyster" refers to the Latin name of the Danube River, not a specific individual.

Similarly, connections between the lives and deaths of American presidents Abraham Lincoln and John F. Kennedy have been suggested, citing coincidences and similarities. However, these connections often arise from selective interpretation rather than genuine prophetic foresight. The Texas Sharpshooter fallacy highlights the human tendency to emphasize connections that fit a narrative while neglecting the broader context and complexity of events.

Self-Fulfilling Prophecy

A self-fulfilling prophecy occurs when an individual predicts an outcome and then intentionally or unintentionally takes actions to make that prediction come true. This can be done by the predictor themselves or by those who have faith in the prophecy.

Renowned author Paulo Coelho explores this idea in his novel "The Alchemist," emphasizing that a strong belief in achieving a goal can influence events to align in one's favor. This belief is a universal trait found in different societies, where conviction and self-assurance often empower individuals to accomplish what they truly believe. This phenomenon extends beyond fiction and literature, manifesting in our everyday lives.

For instance, imagine a teacher who firmly believes that a particular student possesses exceptional intelligence and is destined for academic excellence. Naturally, the teacher devotes more attention, motivation, and support to that student. This goes beyond mere fondness; it becomes essential for the teacher to validate their anticipation and prediction.

At the same time, aware of the teacher's trust and optimism, the student strives to meet and surpass expectations, driven not to disappoint. With favorable circumstances, encouragement, and unwavering determination, the student rises to fulfill the cherished ambitions of the esteemed teacher.

The Making of a Princess

In the UK, a fortune teller once predicted to a mother that her daughter was destined to become a princess. Despite similar forecasts being given by the fortune teller to many others, this particular mother was resolute in her belief that she could shape her daughter's extraordinary destiny. She took the proactive step of enrolling her daughter in the same school as Prince William.

As time progressed, Prince William encountered a girl named Kate Middleton. The mother actively fostered their friendship, seizing every available opportunity to bring them together. Eventually, the prince fell in love with Kate, and they got married. Overnight, the fortune teller gained fame, and her prophecy was hailed as an astonishing example of foresight. Nevertheless, it's possible that the fortune teller had made similar predictions about potential princess status to many others. These prophecies might have been ignored or dismissed by everyone else. What set this situation apart was the mother's unwavering conviction and persistent efforts to make the prophecy come true. This story could be seen as a prime illustration of a self-fulfilling prophecy.

Haunted Houses: Scientific Explanations

Haunted houses have long been a fascination for thrill-seekers and paranormal enthusiasts, fueling countless tales of ghostly encounters and supernatural phenomena. While the allure of haunted houses often stems from the unknown, science and psychology offer intriguing insights into the phenomena commonly associated with these spooky dwellings.

The Power of Perception:

One of the key elements contributing to the haunted house experience is the power of perception. Our brains are wired to detect patterns and make sense of our surroundings, sometimes leading us to interpret random stimuli as something more sinister. This psychological phenomenon, known as pareidolia, can cause individuals to see faces in shadows, hear whispers in the wind, or perceive eerie figures in the darkness.

Environmental Factors:

Many reported haunted houses share common environmental factors that may contribute to the spooky atmosphere. Creaky floorboards, drafty corridors, and flickering lights can create an unsettling ambiance. Moreover, old houses with their unique smells, sounds, and architectural quirks may evoke a sense of nostalgia or eeriness, depending on one's perspective.

Historical Imprints:

Psychologists propose the concept of residual hauntings, suggesting that intense emotional events may leave an imprint on the environment. Traumatic or highly charged experiences in a particular location could influence individuals who later visit the site, making them feel as if they have encountered a ghostly presence.

Unusual Cold Sensations Inside Rooms

Many people have reported feeling an unnatural coldness in specific areas, even when doors and windows are securely closed. What causes this phenomenon? In houses with limited human presence and insufficient lighting, cold air can seep into the space through small gaps or cracks. Additionally, as objects within the room have different temperatures, certain materials release heat through a process called induction. As a result, cooler air flows downward through warmer air openings.

When this chilling current from the damp room brushes against our bodies, combined with the fear of potential hauntings, the sensation becomes even more unsettling. The perception of coldness in these scenarios can lead to the assumption of paranormal activity.

Sounds Beyond the Range of Human Hearing

The human auditory range spans from 20 Hz to 20 kHz in terms of sound perception. Birds and other animals can hear sounds that are too high or low for humans to detect. Pets sometimes react fearfully to sounds that humans cannot hear because they can pick up on these frequencies. Various things can produce sounds that fall outside the human hearing range. These sounds can create vibrations in objects, leading to feelings of fear or unease. Some sound waves can even evoke sensations in the stomach or elicit specific emotions.

Infrasound and Vibrations:

Scientists have explored the role of infrasound, low-frequency vibrations below the range of human hearing, in creating feelings of unease and fear. Some haunted locations are found to have naturally occurring infrasound, which could induce a range of physiological effects, including dizziness, nausea, and heightened anxiety. These subtle vibrations might contribute to the eerie feelings associated with haunted spaces.

Shapes Captured Only in Photographs

In certain haunted houses, there are eerie shapes and distorted images that appear in photographs. These shapes are often caused by small particles of dirt, dust, or insects that come close to the camera lens. The camera lens has the ability to magnify these tiny particles, making them appear as larger objects. This is why strange shapes are sometimes observed in photographs of haunted houses. Creatures that are typically disregarded while taking photos may appear as monstrous entities when captured in an image due to the way the camera lens captures and interprets these minuscule elements.

Expectation and Suggestion

The power of suggestion plays a crucial role in how individuals perceive and interpret their surroundings. When entering a reputedly haunted house, people may already have preconceived notions of encountering ghosts or paranormal activities. This heightened expectation can influence their perceptions and contribute to the creation of haunted narratives.

Deaths in Haunted Houses

Certain vacant houses can give people peculiar experiences if they spend the night there. People may feel lightheaded or even encounter severe health issues. They may start perceiving illusions that aren't real and may even faint before entering.

The main cause behind these frightening occurrences is often old or malfunctioning water heaters, chimneys, furnaces, and cooling systems. These devices can leak dangerous gases, posing a serious health risk that can lead to severe illness or even death. These houses become known for their sorrowful and eerie tales of unfortunate incidents.

Electromagnetic Fields (EMF) and Sensing Ghosts

Dr. Michaels Prasanjir, a Canadian scientist, conducted intriguing experiments revealing that certain types of waves can create a sensation of presence, even if invisible. People's perceptions can vary based on their imagination. It's possible that some electronic devices emit these waves, which could explain why people believe they have encountered ghosts.

Studies have suggested a correlation between paranormal experiences and elevated electromagnetic fields (EMF). Certain locations, including old houses, may have naturally occurring high EMF levels. Prolonged exposure to such fields has been linked to hallucinations, feelings of being watched, and even a sense of dread, providing a plausible explanation for reported ghostly encounters.

Chemicals, Toxins, Mold: Unveiling the Hidden Dangers

Certain types of mold thrive in enclosed and damp spaces. Inhaling their microscopic particles can result in severe illness and hallucinations. Additionally, harmful gases like carbon monoxide and formaldehyde linger in the air, posing significant health risks to individuals.

Mushrooms: A Silent Threat in Closed Spaces

In closed, abundant bungalows, mushrooms grow profusely alongside other plants and potentially poisonous reptiles. Most of these mushrooms harbor poisonous properties. Take, for example, Amanita phalloides, commonly known as the death cap. This deceptive fungus resembles edible mushrooms but is highly toxic. Consuming it can lead to coma and death in over 50 percent of cases. Remarkably, historical fatalities caused by this deadly mushroom include Pope Clement VII in 1534 and Roman Emperor Claudius in 54 CE. In closed environments, the growth of mushrooms can escalate the risks associated with toxic exposure.

22. Near Death Experience: Encounters With Death And Heaven

Dr. Mary Neal, an American orthopedic surgeon, recounts her near-death experience. In 1999, while kayaking in Chile, she and her husband faced death as they drowned. After being unconscious underwater for approximately thirty minutes, they were eventually rescued. During this time, they both had an out-of-body experience and journeyed to heaven. In this divine realm, they encountered God, who delivered the heartbreaking news that their son would soon pass away. Despite this sorrowful revelation, they experienced an overwhelming and lasting sense of joy. Subsequently, Mary Neal's son did indeed pass away.

Now, let us delve into the personal account of Serena, a young woman who lost consciousness following a road accident. Here is what Serena described about her experience:

"I could observe my motionless body in the intensive care unit of the hospital. I was dressed in a blue hospital gown and had a mask on my face, surrounded by complex life support equipment. As I left my body, I ascended and found myself in a dark tunnel, effortlessly floating through it. At the end of this lengthy tunnel, a powerful and brilliant light emanated. My mind felt serene and tranquil, devoid of any sorrow or pain. Outside the tunnel, I sensed a heavenly presence and beheld angels gracefully soaring within that divine light. I also had the privilege of seeing my mother, who had departed two years prior. However, I was eventually compelled to return."

These profound encounters with death and heaven leave us with a profound sense of awe and an insatiable curiosity about the mysteries that lie beyond this earthly existence.

Maria's Near-Death Experience: A Mysterious Shoe and a Hospital Window

Maria's near-death experience began as she lay in the hospital, fighting for her life. Temporarily separated from her physical body, she observed the doctors and nurses diligently working to save her. However, her attention was drawn to an unusual sight—a shoe perched precariously in a third-floor window of the hospital. Intrigued, researchers delved deeper into this enigma.

Further investigation revealed that the shoe was indeed visible from Maria's hospital bed. It is likely that she had noticed it during her admission or overheard conversations about it. The presence of the shoe sparked curiosity and raised questions about the nature of near-death experiences.

While many near-death experiences share common elements, such as feelings of tranquility and visions of radiant light, not all of them are positive or uplifting. Some can be distressing or unsettling. However, these accounts often receive less attention and publicity.

This disparity in attention may stem from readers' preferences. Those seeking stories of hope and reassurance may be less inclined to explore negative or troubling near-death experiences.

As humans, we are naturally inclined to seek comfort and positivity, especially when confronted with the inevitability of mortality.

Near-Death Emotions: Scientific Analysis

Otoscopy - Leaving the Body:

The phenomenon of leaving one's body and venturing beyond is commonly referred to as otoscopy. During these experiences, individuals may feel detached from their physical selves.

Brain Disorders:

The temporoparietal junction in the human brain plays a crucial role in integrating sensory and bodily information to create our sense of self. Even minor disruptions in this brain area can lead to a distorted sense of being outside the body. Scientific experiments have shown that artificially inducing specific brain waves can trigger similar sensations.

Anesthesia:

Many patients describe near-death experience-like sensations upon awakening from anesthesia, both in life-threatening situations and less severe ones. The administration of anesthesia can influence how patients perceive time during sedation.

Out-of-Body Experiences:

Accounts of those who claim to have had out-of-body experiences lack consistent scientific documentation. Often, individuals recount their experiences years after the fact, and the manner in which interviewers frame their questions can influence their storytelling.

Oxygen Deprivation:

Episodes of oxygen deprivation in the bloodstream, such as during cardiac arrest, falls from heights, or near-drowning incidents, can lead to hallucinations and illusions. Reduced oxygen levels may result in experiences such as seeing loved ones, angels, or hearing divine voices.

Body Chemistry and Hormones:

Intense stress can trigger the release of hormones like endorphins, which induce feelings of tranquility, pleasure, and affection. Near-death situations could stimulate the production of endorphins, potentially causing visions of heavenly realms.

Hormonal Imbalances:

Certain medical conditions affecting hormone regulation can cause delusions and mental disturbances, leading to perceptions like encountering spirits or feeling a lifeless body.

Higher Carbon Dioxide Levels:

Elevated carbon dioxide levels in the bloodstream can affect vision and contribute to hallucinations, including tunnel vision and sightings of bright lights.

Temporal Lobe Epilepsy:

Temporal lobe epilepsy is a condition characterized by seizures originating in the temporal lobes of the brain. These seizures can cause various sensory and perceptual disturbances, including delusions and vivid visions. Interestingly, not all cases of temporal lobe epilepsy are recognized as such, and some people may interpret their experiences through a spiritual lens.

For individuals with spiritual tendencies or a predisposition to heightened emotions, their encounters may prompt medical professionals to consider temporal lobe epilepsy. Diagnosis can be derived from brainwave tests like electroencephalographs conducted during these altered perception moments.

Remarkably, historical figures such as Joan of Arc and Fyodor Dostoevsky were later identified as having suffered from temporal lobe epilepsy. Dostoevsky's description of his spiritual encounter, where he felt deeply connected to his body and the universe, is a poignant illustration of these experiences. He expressed a willingness to sacrifice a significant portion of his life for the fleeting moments of euphoria he felt during these episodes.

Factors Influencing Near-Death Experiences

Near-death experiences are not universally reported by all individuals who have faced death and survived. Instead, they are more commonly described by individuals with tendencies towards delusions, spiritual inclinations, or mental health conditions. It is important to note that experiencing a near-death episode does not necessarily indicate a life-threatening situation.

During these experiences, individuals often encounter vivid and imaginative scenes. These scenes are shaped by various factors, including personal backgrounds, cultural influences, religious beliefs, past life experiences, and even individual desires. It is crucial to acknowledge that these experiences are highly subjective and unique to each person who undergoes them.

A Neurosurgeon's Near-Death Experience:

Dr. Ibn Alexander, a neurosurgeon, shared a personal account of his near-death experience while in a coma caused by meningitis. During this coma, the normal functioning of his cerebral cortex, responsible for memories, thoughts, language, and sensory perceptions, ceased. His experience has sparked discussions about the potential existence of an afterlife.

However, Dr. Oliver Sacks, a renowned neurosurgeon and professor, offers a plausible explanation for this phenomenon. He explains that near-death sensations typically last for a brief period, usually around twenty to thirty seconds. However, due to the altered state of consciousness, these moments can subjectively feel much longer, even stretching into minutes or hours. When in an unconscious state, the perception of time becomes distorted, making it challenging to determine whether these experiences are genuine or mere illusions. As a result, individuals are more inclined to view these encounters as authentic and meaningful.

Part V. Unconventional Paths To Success

23. Embracing Boredom

"Mom, I'm bored... Can I watch cartoons? I have nothing to do, should I play a game?" These are common questions children often ask, seeking electronic entertainment. On the other hand, parents may wonder how their children can find time to play amidst their busy schedules. Sometimes, giving them an iPad or electronic device can seem like a convenient solution.

But should we really worry about boredom? Do we feel proud when our kids master electronic gadgets? Let's explore the true impact of boredom on children's mental development.

In every civilized society, there is a belief that children should always be engaged in activities and not be idle. However, modern psychological research offers interesting insights into boredom.

Studies conducted by Dr. Sandy Mann of the University of Lancashire, Dr. Teresa Belten of the University of East Anglia, and others reveal that engaging in relatively boring and repetitive activities actually stimulates creative and innovative thinking in children.

A study published by the University of Texas in 2013 suggests that boredom, loneliness, and idleness redirect mental energy towards more productive, useful, and imaginative pursuits.

Similarly, a study from the University of California found that wandering minds are not signs of laziness; they increase mental energy and nurture the ability to analyze problems holistically and find solutions. Boredom can be a blessing in disguise.

Let's explore five blessings that boredom can bring to children based on the above findings:

Children learn that happiness and joy do not always come from external sources. Instead of always focusing on screens, encourage them to observe and understand the world around them - people, animals, and things. This fosters independent thinking and mental independence.

Boredom can boost children's creativity. Studies show that daydreaming and imagination are closely connected. When bored, the mind wanders, and imagination takes flight. Nurturing their imaginations can make them stronger over time.

Boredom relieves stress. Constantly staring at fast-blinking screens can stress a child's brain, leading to eye problems and a lack of physical exercise.

By allowing children to experience moments of boredom, we can help them develop creativity, resilience, and problem-solving skills. Instead of fearing boredom, let's embrace it as an opportunity for growth and development in our children's lives.

24. An Alternative Approach To Success

Failure-Based Model

India's lunar exploration satellite, Chandrayaan-3, was successfully launched on July 14, 2023, from Sriharikota, Andhra Pradesh. The Chief of the Indian Space Research Organisation (ISRO), S. Somnath, revealed that they have adopted a failure-based model to ensure the success of Chandrayaan-3.

This approach involves identifying potential points of failure and implementing measures to prevent them. The "Failure-Based Model" focuses on learning from failures and mistakes, which is a concept applied in various fields such as education, business, personal development, and psychology. Instead of solely focusing on success, this model emphasizes the importance of understanding the reasons for failure. It provides valuable lessons, insights, and growth opportunities that ultimately lead to success.

In a failure-based model, failure is not a reason to give up. Instead, it is seen as a stepping stone towards progress. This model helps individuals and organizations to absorb failures, analyze their causes, and make better decisions based on the knowledge gained. It encourages taking more effective actions in the future.

Let's delve into the key aspects of the failure-based model:

Failures are seen as opportunities for learning and self-improvement. By analyzing what went wrong and why, individuals can identify areas for growth and implement necessary changes.

Addressing failures directly prepares individuals to avoid repeating those mistakes. Those who learn from failure become more resilient in the face of setbacks and develop strategies to overcome challenges.

Failure-based models foster innovative thinking. While experiments and risks may result in failures, they often lead to significant discoveries and creative solutions.

This model encourages the "Growth Mindset," reinforcing the belief that skills and intelligence can be cultivated through effort and learning. People with this mindset view failures as temporary obstacles.

Incorporating lessons from failures into future endeavors allows individuals and organizations to continuously enhance their performance and efficiency.

It's important to note that while the failure-based model is valuable and inspiring, success doesn't solely depend on failure. Factors such as effective planning, skills, persistence, and a supportive environment also contribute to achieving goals. Additionally, it's crucial to discern between valuable learning experiences and unproductive failures. Not all failures offer constructive insights, as some may stem from poor decisions or uncontrollable circumstances. Therefore, the ability to differentiate between the two is essential.

Let's embrace flexibility:

There is a management theory called the contingency approach, and this principle can be applied to life as well. As self-help experts often emphasize, there is no one-size-fits-all solution. People have diverse life circumstances, so a single approach won't work universally. The same applies to behavior. Treating everyone the same isn't always optimal.

Our methods should be adjusted based on individual differences, situations, ages, and stages of life. However, it can be challenging for individuals to remain adaptable and avoid becoming overly inflexible in any particular way.

The Law of the Instrument

"If the only tool you have is a hammer, you tend to see every problem as a nail." This well-known quote is attributed to the renowned Harvard psychologist, Prof. Abraham Maslow. This concept is also known as the 'law of instrument' or Maslow's hammer. It refers to an excessive reliance on a familiar or preferred tool, which can also apply to ideas and beliefs.

When we try to solve a problem or accomplish a task, we often limit ourselves to using a specific skill or tool that we are comfortable with. This can result in investing a significant amount of time and effort in solving a problem using only one predefined method. While it is true that continually using the same skill or tool can improve our proficiency, it can also hinder us from acquiring other skills, making us less effective overall.

This issue is most evident in the education system. Every child has unique talents and weaknesses. The notion that they can all absorb the same information at the same pace and using the same approach is irrational. Yet, this is the prevailing educational approach in our country. Many educators fail to recognize that each student has distinct capabilities, and not everyone can excel in every subject. Is it fair to label an elephant as inferior to a monkey just because it can't climb trees?

Déformation professionnelle

Déformation professionnelle is a French term that describes a cognitive bias where individuals perceive the world solely through the lens of their profession. Self-help gurus often promote rigid approaches like these, which can lead to limited thinking. The self-help industry sometimes encourages people to adopt a mechanistic lifestyle, constantly striving for personal development. This creates a culture where individuals feel the need to continuously improve themselves and their lives, believing that their current state is inherently incomplete.

When experts in a specific field try to apply their expertise universally, it can result in the déformation professionnelle bias. It is not appropriate for a doctor to think like a physicist, and vice versa, as they face distinct challenges in their respective domains. Employing a one-size-fits-all approach will never be effective for companies or laboratories that require diverse areas of expertise.

Einstellung Effect

Another bias that can contribute to the limited thinking described by the law of instrumentality is the Einstellung effect.

This effect involves our tendency to rely on past experiences as the solution to all problems. Needless to say, this phenomenon is closely related to the self-help industry and its promotion of rigid approaches.

Success is the result of accumulative advantages that happen in life.

ABOUT THE AUTHOR

Dr. Robin K Mathew is a psychologist and ethnographer—a social psychology analyst contributing to various media platforms. His journey unfolds as a tapestry woven with rich experiences and profound insights. With a career spanning the globe, he has had the privilege of engaging with individuals from nearly 90 different nationalities, each representing a mosaic of socio-economic, ethnic, and linguistic backgrounds.

Having academic qualifications and working experience in areas such as Information Technology, Human Resource Management, Psychology, Cyber Psychology, Dr. Mathew has worked and associated with various prestigious organizations in various capacities. These include the University of Toronto, Best Buy, The Indian Institute of Management, ICFAI Business School, the Royal Bank of Canada, and Michigan University, among others.

This extensive exposure has cultivated a diverse understanding of human behavior and life in its myriad forms. Over the past twelve years, Dr. Mathew's written work has found a home in several prestigious magazines, both in India and abroad. To date, he has authored close to 500 articles across a wide spectrum of subjects, infusing each piece with the wisdom and insight gained through his work.

Additionally, Dr. Mathew has successfully authored and published 14 books, each offering a unique exploration of diverse facets of human psychology and the human condition.

Other books by the Author:

Mayalam

1. Madamballiyile Manorogik
2. Digital Nagavallim
3. Manasu Vazhi thettikkunna 101 Reethik
4. Jeevitha Vijayathinte Krithrima Thakk
5. Cyber Parakaya Pravesh
6. Kaanan Desham Theti Pokunnav
7. Chekuthante Panipu
8. Chanakyante Kamukim

English

1. I am Akira
2. The Psychology of mind Decepti
3. Lovers of Chanak
4. In the Quest of the Promised La
5. The Expedition of a N

Email: robinkmathew@gmail.com

Writer's Pocket

Writer's Pocket is a publication house established in 2016. We began with the aim of providing a better publishing platform for aspiring writers and budding poets.

The publishing industry in India (and around the world, to a great extent) is always something of a mystery even to the writers themselves. We are working on making publishing more accessible to everyone.

So far, we have helped over 3,000 writers turn their dreams into reality by publishing the books and continue to do so. By doing so, we also provide some of the best content by Indian writers to the readers.

Want to read more books? Scan this QR code with your smartphone and check out all our books on Amazon.